Copyright © 2019 Alex DiFrancesco
All rights reserved.
Typesetting by Marina Garcia
Cover Art by Jam Jacobs
Cover Design by Janice Lee
Copyediting by Chiwan Choi
ISBN 978-1-948700-13-9

THE ACCOMPLICES:
A Civil Coping Mechanisms Book

theaccomplices.org

THE ACCOMPLICES

PSYCHOPOMPS

by Alex DiFrancesco

for Vivien Ryder, Jessie Rose Lee, Ron Kuby, and Adam Wishneusky, all of whom have provided support that this book would not be possible without. This dedication is a mere token that will never match the reality of their kindness.

"Those songs that speak of love without having within in their lines an ache or a sigh are not love songs at all but rather Hate Songs disguised as love songs, and are not to be trusted."
—Nick Cave, "The Secret Life of the Love Song"

"Never lament casually."
—Leonard Cohen, on what he learned from Lorca

Georgette

1.

I am in an introductory fiction writing class in college in New York City, and we are tasked with bringing in a paragraph we find particularly moving. This is my first semester at the small liberal arts college that I was accepted to after finishing community college in Nanticoke, PA. It is after my nervous breakdowns have started, and before I will know who I am. In a few weeks, I will go to a school psychologist who will ask me what I like about a book I am reading, and I will reply, "I like characters who change drastically." He will refer me to a trans-identity clinic. I won't go, thinking that he clearly doesn't understand me. It will be years until I can accept myself.

    I choose the paragraph from Hubert Selby, Jr.'s *Last Exit to Brooklyn* in which a transgender sex worker, Georgette, saves the atmosphere of a party by pulling down a book and reading Poe's "The Raven" aloud as Charlie Parker echoes from the record player. I don't then know why this section makes me cry. Perhaps, I think, it is because Poe was my first love, literature in general my second, and despair in literature my third.

We go around the room, reading from Carver, Bowles, and Cheever. We never get to Georgette's shining moment.

At a later date, in the same class, we are assigned to write a short piece in which one of the characters has a secret. A boy in the class who is, by self-description, straight and cisgender writes a scene in which a transgender woman is hiding her gender identity from her lover. The big reveal is her final pronoun, which he writes as "s/he."

2.

I am on my way to a folk songshare with my friend Ellis, from college. We stop in an East Village garden, and they rub a buttercup under my chin, informing me that my chin is glowing, and it means I will fall in love. I meet a bartender at the dive bar where the folk music event takes place. I think, "He's the kind of guy I would sleep with once, then never talk to again."

On our second date, after sex, the bartender tells me that though she appears to the world as a cisgender male, she identifies as "spiritually transgender." We talk about our childhoods, and it becomes painfully clear to me that I shared all the hallmarks of a transgender child. I think about the years between then and now: my obsession with transgender people in literature and film; my determination to make friends with the one transgender person in my small hometown for reasons I couldn't at the time understand; my fascination with David Bowie and Lou Reed, the closest access I have to such people in art.

I don't know any trans people other than the bartender and me. I go to the library, which has never failed me. I turn back to the books I grew up with like *Last Exit* while also reading more modern gender scholars and specialists like Kate Bornstein, Riki Wilchins, Judith Butler, and Julia Serrano. I begin to understand why Georgette made me cry.

3.

My Bachelor's degree in creative writing has landed me the only kind of job it probably ever will. I work in the office of a bookstore. My boss is the guy who wrote the "s/he" reveal all those years ago. I wonder if he remembers? I remember. I am not out at work.

Coworkers friend me on Facebook. They see my chosen name, which I still haven't been able to start using at work. They see my identification as transgender. Some of them are kind. There is the man with the long, white beard who I have seen in this bookstore since the first time I came in years ago, David. He asks me if I would prefer to be called Alex. His kindness breaks the aloof persona that I have affected for protection. But mostly, I eat lunch alone and write. One day someone tells me they would talk to me more, but that I have "an air of solitude."

I read *Last Exit to Brooklyn* critically. With a growing circle of transgender friends, many of them writers, with access to books written by transgender people, I see every one of the reductive tropes. Sad sex worker. Tragic heroin addict. Death. Exactly what every last cisgender person makes of transgender women in literature. I don't think deeply about the fact that many of the trans people I know *do* in fact do some kind of sex work to get by in New York—myself included, taking off my clothes on webcams and acting out men's fantasies on pay-per-hour phone lines. Or that a lot of us struggle with drinking and drugs. I think: This is wrong. This is problematic. Why do cis people keep portraying trans people this way? Even recent books such as *Adam* by Ariel Schrag have kept up the legacy of transness as cis foil.

I marry the bartender, who has transitioned with my support. I work at the bookstore for two years, and towards the end of my employment, she leaves me. I start drinking hard, wallowing in depression, and missing work. I get doctor's notes from the nurses at my trans specific clinic that use my chosen name. The guy who wrote the "s/he" reveal sits me down in his office. The walls don't go up to the ceiling, and everyone outside his office, in the larger office area, can hear every word. He talks about how I am no longer a reliable employee, and, anyway, what is going on with these notes being under a name that's not even mine?

4.

I sit down to write this essay, and in doing so, pull up the paragraph that describes Georgette's moment of beauty. There are so many things wrong with this book. We can write our own stories so much better than those who use us to glimpse what it's like on the outside. But as I read, I see Selby writing with as much compassion as I could expect him to. The other characters look at Georgette as a man, as themselves as gay for their attraction to her. Selby never does—Selby sees Georgette as she wants to be seen. And though he kills Georgette, he first gives her this moment that is the most that any of his characters could hope for—harsh poetry.

There is so much I could have used, years before, that none of these books or any of the songs like "Walk on the Wild Side" ever gave me. Any sort of transmasculine person in literature or art, any sort of voice from someone much more like myself, any sort of positive portrayal of trans people. Someone saying that things will be a mess and a disaster, and, also, quite inexplicably, okay.

Again, at the moment of Georgette's death, I am crying.

How to Disappear

In 2016, in New York City, a 19-year-old engineering student named Nayla Kidd disappeared. She changed bank accounts, cell phone providers, shut down her social media, and ditched her Ivy League college to move to Bushwick and become an artist and model, all without informing anyone in her life. Social media jumped all over the story, and then news outlets latched on. Kidd was a missing person for around two weeks when the police finally found her.

    I read her post-discovery missive in *The New York Post*, which described her fancy boarding school, full scholarship to Columbia University, calculated plans, the loving mom who had clearly sacrificed for her. I thought it was a story of absolute callousness. She'd had everything, but she said the pressure was too much, that she'd wanted to run away and have the fun life she saw in an East Williamsburg loft she was thinking of renting. I remember reading it, sitting there and staring at the words while thinking of my own picture plastered across subways and bus stations. How could she do such a thing intentionally? Didn't she understand what it was like to be truly lost?

Perhaps I was jealous of the attention she received. When my mental illness made me a missing person in 2010, the NYPD suggested to my friends who reported me missing that I had run off to follow a band. Though my friends set up a cross-country network of activists looking for me in any of the places they thought I might have been, the NYPD did little. Had the cops accessed my bank account, or even looked at my Metrocard swipes (an investigation practice well-established by law enforcement by 2010), they'd have easily figured out that I wandered around the city for days before taking a bus to my hometown and checking myself into a hospital.

When I saw Kidd's story, I thought of all the resources that had gone into her "case," and all of those of us who really were lost, unhealthy, and scared, who were given little to no help.

Alone in a hospital bed that year, unknown, technically still "missing," my head still a wash of paranoia and confusion, I began to entertain a fantasy. What if I moved to the Midwest? Changed my name? My gender? Grew a beard? I couldn't remember ever thinking thoughts like this, but just then I had a vision of myself, flat-chested, wearing a white Hanes T-shirt, a genderless pair of Levis, and combat boots. What if I disappeared from my life? Started over as someone new? I was not well at the time—I was also standing in front of the mirror thinking about a bug I was certain had entered into my skin and been living in my bloodstream for years, something I now know is not true—but since I had succeeded in disappearing from everyone in my life, I wondered, "What if I really need to disappear?"

It wasn't until years later when I remembered this fantasy that I began to empathize with Nayla Kidd.

At the time I became a missing person, I was fairly happy with my life—not when I thought about it too much, not when the things I couldn't control took control of me, but fairly happy. At 28, I had just graduated the college I had dreamed of attending when I was 18, where I'd studied creative writing on a hefty scholarship. I had a group of socially engaged, politically aware activist friends whom I considered a family. Though my relationship with my blood family had been strained by my mental illness over the prior few years, I knew that they loved me, even if they couldn't understand me. Well, that was what I kept telling myself.

I didn't consciously feel there was any reason for me to disappear.

It had been less than six months since my last nervous breakdown, which occurred around Christmas time, 2009, after I had just finished finals, and my mother and brother came to New York from Pennsylvania to pick me up for holiday break. They had driven from my hometown, a dilapidated former coal-mining town called Wilkes-Barre, the county-seat in a small Northern Appalachian valley, to my apartment at the end of Brooklyn, near Coney Island.

The minute I got into the car, my brother said something unabashedly racist. I remember putting my head against the cold window and shutting down. I'd been going to a really progressive college, I had learned so much, and my family said things like this. They believed my mental illness was "fake," little more than me "looking for attention." I rode the whole way home in silence, and, then, curled up in my old bed, fell apart.

At one point during the next few, awful days, I began talking to my mom about whether I was a boy or a girl. She yelled that she had never heard of such a thing, that I was talking like a crazy person.

"What the fuck is wrong with you?" my older brother screamed. "Do you want mom to have a heart attack? Do you want me to have one? If she does, I'll fucking kill you. I'll break you in fucking half. I'll fucking kill you." It would not be the last time he would threaten my life.

After that break, once I got out of the hospital, I returned to school, and didn't engage much with my blood family. I called them occasionally, I felt bound to them, but I began removing myself from their lives as best I could. By May 2010—the time I disappeared—we were speaking less and less.

◇◇

It's now been seven years since my last mental breakdown, and thinking of the state that made me run away from my life is not easy. I feel shame and guilt over inappropriate things I'd said or done years before. There had been elaborate paranoid constructions based on biographies I'd read of Brian Wilson. There had been mild visual and auditory hallucinations. Walking down the street, I'd imagined I was in a *Truman Show*-like reality program, and the high-pitched tweets I heard in the sky were drones following and filming me. These are hard memories to return to, even harder because, as anyone who has left sanity for a time knows, a door once opened is never quite shut. Though I no longer live in fear of losing reality, the possibility remains like a cracked door's edge of light in a dark room.

During my breakdowns, there was also some of the most beautiful art I will ever create—two of my early published short stories were written from the depths of these mental hells, in hospitals. I would carry papers with me, ignore the therapeutic activities, scribble down the scenes that had flitted across my brain while I went in and out of my mind, and the sense I'd try to make of them through fiction.

In spring 2010, having just graduated college, I was planning on moving to Mexico to teach ESL. My chosen family of activists and I had just crossed an international border to attend a huge protest for a G20 summit. We ran from the police through parks in the night time with helicopters over our heads. We were arrested. By the time we got back home to New York City, I saw danger everywhere. I was in a very bad place.

Everyone in my life hated me, I was sure. Even as I curled up, unshowered and deeply depressed, on a friend's couch while my friends tried to care for me, I was positive that there was something intrinsically unlovable about me, unequivocally wrong, and that any day, those around me would find out. Every relationship in my life was built on a lie, I was sure.

    I left the couch for an appointment with my therapist. But I'd gotten the day wrong and the clinic was closed. This confirmed everything I was thinking—everyone hated me, they were pushing me out, I was locked out. I sent some cryptic texts to my friends and left my cell phone at a bus stop so I wouldn't have to answer any more calls from people I was convinced had discarded me.

    Confused, depressed, and suicidal, I wandered around Coney Island, then took a train to the end of the 7 line in Queens. I tried to sleep on a subway bench, and the cops harassed me until I left. By this time, a day or two later, my friends had accepted that involving police—usually no activist's best friend—was the only way they might find me. While one NYPD officer was telling them I'd probably run off with a band, another was poking me with his baton and telling me to move along. I spent days being hustled from one place to another before I finally got on a bus, sick and sweaty and barely able to maintain any semblance of normalcy, and headed for my hometown, where I checked myself into a hospital.

◇◇

    It was in the blue plastic bed of that hospital with its scratchy white sheets that I began to imagine a life completely unlike my own. I could escape and start over. I could be a different person. Mexico wasn't far enough. I had an old Metro North ticket receipt in my pocket that I kept looking at. It said THIS IS NOT A TICKET FOR TRAVEL, and I took it as a sign that this receipt was there with me for a reason. It meant that I couldn't go away geographically but keep the rest of my life the same. There had to be a clean break, a chance to start over completely.

As my medications kicked in, the thoughts began to clear. In a few days, I picked up the telephone and called my mother, who broke down in tears.

Shortly after that, my mother had a stroke, which my family blamed on my disappearance. My brother threatened to kill me again, and the bonds that I'd been holding onto were finally broken. I haven't seen them in eight years.

My mental health is stable now. I believe a great number of the things that haunted me—paranoia, feeling others would see me as I couldn't see myself and judge me unlovable—were relieved when I finally came out as transgender. It was not an easy process. I had fallen in love with another person, Mya, who was realizing slowly that she was transgender, and so many memories I'd blocked out came flooding back to me as we talked about our identities. Having someone understand me, love me, and support my gender identity let me be the person that I'd been hiding from myself, the too much and too far that some of the people who had said they'd loved me all my life couldn't allow. Some people did look at the real me and judge me as unlovable. Others adapted, learned, embraced.

I don't think that everyone who goes missing is hiding such a deep secret. But when I think about that liminal space—where we can be invisible to those who make us who we are—I understand why we run.

When I read Nayla Kidd's story, I saw someone who had everything, but wanted it to be more, different, and exactly what she chose. Don't we all deserve that, though, to a degree? At times, I told myself it was enough for me to be the person I had become because of the pressure on me, but deep down, it wasn't. My psyche wouldn't allow it. And instead of making calculated moves, I made myself ill. The end result was the same. She ran. I ran.

I'm currently living in the Midwest, with a new name and a new gender, growing a beard. I didn't have to shed everyone in my life to do this. But maybe it had helped to disappear briefly. I wonder whether I would have made all these major, vital changes toward becoming a truer version of myself if I hadn't taken the space from everyone—if I hadn't had a momentary look at what my life might be if I were the only one choosing.

Genealogy (Part One): Ancestry

Before we are married, Mya and I are staying in her aunt's West Village apartment after her aunt suffered a stroke that will preclude her from ever returning to it. I decide I want to understand where I came from. Perhaps it is the dour, sullen-eyed ancestors whose pictures her aunt has hanging on every wall. I don't know why they stand out more than everything else—more than the small pieces of broken things the aunt keeps in dishes, the lighted bathroom mirror in which we pose for selfies with "FAG" and "DYKE" written across our faces in red lipstick. But I cannot sleep there, under those eyes. I stay up late, looking for where I came from.

Ancestry.com is a scam for lazy dilettantes of the genealogy world. You can find the same things for free if you dig just a bit further. I google and I google and I google, and eventually I find the ship record from when my paternal grandmother, Assunta Donato, came to America. This is a woman I have never met. The only things I know about her are (1) that she died from falling down the basement stairs while trying to carry the vacuum up them and (2) she had the same lack of right and left lateral teeth that I had. My father had unwisely told me this on the day we learned I had to get braces to correct the anomaly, to comfort me. My mother, faced with a packet of bill reminders the size of a car payment, had screamed at him about his bad genes.

When I come across the handwritten ship log, staticky with internet replication and age, I see that the name her parents registered her with was "Assuntina," little Assunta. She was two. I picture this small girl on a big ship, her teeth still perfect little baby teeth, the gap that will proclaim her poverty for the rest of her life lurking somewhere that no one can yet see.

Assuntina. A small, curly haired child, moving toward the prospect of a new world, unsure, but unafraid, with her family, holding their hands. My wife is sleeping, snoring. I get teary. Tears are a theme.

We find out from a neighbor who doesn't know we're trans (very few people do at this point) that, years ago, the aunt's apartment was inhabited by transgender sex workers. They had lived there as a family. It is the Christopher Street Pier. A piece of history renovated and sanitized.

Late at night, Mya talks about how they are her ancestors. She talks about how they talk to her at night. I don't say anything (I know better than to), but the idea terrifies me. I don't want her to be spoken to by the ghosts of people whose lives were constantly in danger, who banded together for safety. I want her to have her mom in New Jersey, who loves her, her vicious sister who loves her, who screamed at me for throwing away a tampon in her bathroom garbage can the first time I went to their house. These people hate me. They think I am low class and unworthy. But they love Mya. Let her have the soft, stable, suburban life I never did. The outcasts, they are my people by necessity. I want softer, safer for her, this person I love, and I am afraid.

No one knows what happened to my uncle Danny. He died before I was born, before my parents were married. On my parents' wedding day, my father's sister pulled my mother aside and said, "No one ever told you what really happened to Danny, did they?" My mother said she didn't want to know. So none of us ever knew.

For years, I fantasized about find the truth, maybe writing about it. I knew one thing, that my Uncle Danny had been awarded a Purple Heart, which we kept in an orange cabinet in our garage that we referred to as Mary's Cabinet, the way other people refer to the claw-foot chair or the Chippendale dressing table. There had to be records. I would find them. When I was diagnosed with bipolar disorder, I began to fantasize that Uncle Danny was mentally ill, and died by his own hand. When I came out as queer, I began to fantasize that he was, too, and was killed in hate crime.

Somehow, Uncle Danny must be the missing link that fit me into the family that had discarded me.

◇◇

I never found out what killed Uncle Danny. I gave up, like a dilettante.

◇◇

My paternal grandfather was a coal miner, which, if you ever ask me what my grandfather did, is what I will tell you.

My maternal grandfather was a bourgeois shit. His family capitalized off of the alcoholism of the miners in the Anthracite mining town I am from, owning a bar that catered to them. When my grandmother and he fell in love, his sisters called her "the doctor bill" because of how poor she was, how they equated poverty with sickness. They chided him for bringing an extra expense to the family. For years, she faced their judgement stoically, responding with regular visits, home-cooked meals when they grew older, and bringing her grandchildren to see them without so much as a word until we were much older on how they had treated her.

In her 80s, when I was still just a child, one of my grandfather's sisters had a stroke, and my grandmother walked with her every day until she regained her strength. The sister, after decades of cruelty, finally understood my grandmother's kindness.

I am not my grandmother.

Mya's grandfather was the inventor of a form of modern pain management. When he died, his obituary ran in *The New York Times*. This used to be in her Wikipedia bio, which she curates obsessively. Her mom grew up with servants, and she owns several pieces of expensive art that her grandmother gave to her. Since she ran away with someone else, moved into an art squat, and joined a trans art club that makes bats for what they call "cis-bashing," she has taken this bit of information off of her page.

◇◇

The first time I had dinner with Mya's family was Passover. When we talked about overcoming oppression, I talked about the Black Panthers, and how, in what was often considered their best achievement, they fed school children who hadn't eaten all day so they could learn without being distracted by their hunger. Later, Mya's mom would tell her that I was "too radical." I spent a lot of that weekend nervous, taking walks, not myself. Their judgment was stifling, as it would continue to be for four years. Mya broke up with me for the first time then. Years later, she would tell the story in front of all of our friends of a nervous habit I had engaged in (chewing the end of a string on one of my hoodies), and how she and her mom and sister had laughed about how she was dating a goat after I left.

◇◇

When I met Mya, I had people around me that I considered family. They were anarchists and activists that I had met as an undergraduate student. We loved each other in all-consuming and often unhealthy ways. We wanted to make a new world. Often, we just ended up flipping old hierarchies. Those of us who society had abused often found we could spin this abuse to hold over the people closest to us—and sometimes we did. Power structures weren't subverted, they just got turned upside down. A lot of us are still recovering from the wreckage of this.

Years later, after Mya is gone, I will sit down with two of the friends who had been my family in those days. We will talk about the years that had passed, and the years in which we didn't speak. One of my friends will tell me that years ago, I had looked her in the eye, and said, "Don't make me choose between you and Mya, because I will choose her."

It is true that Mya did once say the same to her family about me. A few days before she left me for someone else, she sent her mom an email that said, "If you continue to behave the way you are to my spouse, you will lose me." A few days later, she was in motels and Airbnb's with her new partner while I googled ways to die.

◇◇

After I find the ship records, Mya and I agree that we will name our child Sunny, a perfectly gender-neutral derivative of Assunta, even though we are fully aware that her mom would pitch a fit if her grandchild was named after Mary's ascension into heaven, and hormone replacement therapy has made it unlikely we will ever have children. We'll foster at first, we say, one of the older queer kids who's been thrown out of their homes for being queer. Eventually we'll adopt.

On the morning that Mya smashes my favorite coffee cup in a temper tantrum, I know that this will never happen, either.

◇◇

Under the eyes of Mya's ancestors' pictures, I picture little Assunta, Assuntina, who I never met and never knew, on a boat so much bigger than her, the ghost of my own twelve-year-old gap-toothed smile somewhere in her head.

Hank Williams is Sacred

Tai is the first person I ever meet who is a fan of my work. Or who even knows my work exists, really.

They come to one of Mya's shows. Mya had a lot of shows where she played guitar and sang, most of them at venues like the one I used to scorn years before while I walked to the radical bookstore down the street. I didn't like all the shallow-looking people tripping over high heels and loosening their ties out front, cordoned-off from the street by long velvet ropes. It seemed like hell. I am to find myself in this venue quite frequently after marrying Mya.

If you want to see me, at the time, there is a pretty good chance I will be at Mya's shows. All of them. Expected. Sitting in the front row. She doesn't think of me as an ornament, she tells me over and over.

Mya always said she fell in love with me when I invited her to an Occupy Wall Street rally and she hugged me and put one of her hands on the back of my shaved head to pull me close to her, but I don't think it was until she read one of my short stories that she had much respect for me. I didn't take her seriously as a musician until we were driving through Brooklyn and she played me the opening, dark track of her new album on her car stereo. I asked her who it was, because she put it on out of nowhere. She said it was her, and I realized she knew what she was doing.

One of Mya's shows at the venue with the velvet ropes is where Tai comes to see me.

They are tall and waif-thin, with long blond hair and the slightly hunched shoulders of someone who wishes they were much shorter. They are beautiful, and I don't know why they are talking to me, not Mya, congratulating me on my recently published novel, congratulating me on getting my work "out of the trans ghetto." I know them from a trans writing group that most of the people I know circle in and out of. They love my book, they say. They are frustrated with trans writing communities that focus on identity above craft, above literary experimentation. They would like to talk about it all. They would like to talk to me more.

I mutter something awkwardly and run away. My game plan on nights like this is to talk to everyone a little bit, just long enough so they won't see how incredibly uncomfortable I am.

◇◇

I've always been a fan of sad music, but it is when Mya leaves that I become obsessed with break up albums. With what they mean as a cultural artifact, if they will continue to exist as everything becomes digital releases and playlists. I think about the year when I was in my early twenties and faced my first major heartbreak, and Bob Dylan's *Blood on the Tracks* nursed me through it. I had a cassette tape of it that a friend had bought me from a bargain bin in the late '90s when CDs were what we listened to most. I listened to it in the tape deck of my fifteen-year-old Chevy Blazer because I didn't have anywhere else I could play it. It would wind through one side, flip, wind through the next, on and on.

It wouldn't be fair to say that there was ever a time when I *didn't* listen to heartbreak albums—the song I sang for Mya at our wedding was the opening track off of Nick Cave's breakup album, *The Boatman's Call*—but they become my security blanket and obsession in the months after Mya's departure. Mya accidentally left behind the amphetamines that she took for ADHD when she took off, and, even though I have been sober off of everything but alcohol for years, I take them and go to parties and talk about all my research and the book I am going to write on the cultural history of the breakup album.

Frank Sinatra wrote what's often considered the prototypical breakup album. He was allegedly kind of an asshole who treated women like objects, and then expected them to keep him from being lonely. He was still married to his first wife when he met Ava Gardner, who became his second wife. When she left him after he cheated on her repeatedly, he released *In The Wee Small Hours of the Morning*. He mourns and moans his way through a whole album of loneliness, one of the first concept albums ever.

I can't really listen to this album without thinking of my dad, a radio DJ who loved Frank Sinatra, and who split up with my mom when I was two, but remained in my life until he died when I was nineteen. But it's the first of its kind, and it's important to my research, so I listen to it over and over. As much as I don't like Sinatra, it makes me feel a connection to my dad to listen to him, and this is something I cherish when it happens.

It's also a fact that sadness restarted Sinatra's career, which was then failing as the playboy aged out of his teenybopper fanbase. Sadness sells. There are a lot of mourners.

A few weeks after Mya leaves me, I host a party that is to become a video blog for my writers' group's now-defunct web page. Everyone in attendance is going to get very, very drunk and, cold read James Joyce's dirty letters to his wife, Nora, in celebration of Bloomsday. I actually don't like James Joyce at all, but have always believed these filthy letters full of scatological references are the pinnacle of his work. Because I am very poor, I get a huge jug of cheap gin, limes, and several bottles of tonic. Many of the people in attendance will never get sicker than we get that night, due to the horror that is cheap liquor.

Tai is at the party. Tai had been around a lot since Mya disappeared, reaching out, wanting to work on projects, leaving me messages on Facebook. One of them says that, although they are sorry I'm so heartbroken, they are also bracing themself for the amazing art that's going to come out of that heartbreak. After we get drunk and finish making videos of the letters, Tai and a woman I work with and I all end up in my bed.

The next day, still sick, the three of us will call off of work. I mean, maybe I can't blame the guy who wrote the s/he reveal for sitting me down and talking to me. Tai will be fired from their dog walking job, and the woman I work with will have finally run through the graces our union provides workers at the bookstore. The woman will leave, and I will feed Tai cheese, bread, and cured meats to ward off the hangover that is amplified by detoxing off of Suboxone in preparation for the first half of their gender affirming surgery.

I go away to the Catskills for the summer. While I am gone, I listen to *The Boatman's Call* every day. This album was one of the first CDs I bought when I got hired at a used record store in the early '00s. It was released in 1997, and marked a stark departure from previous albums for Nick Cave and the Bad Seeds. Their prior work, and Cave's work with the post-punk band The Birthday Party, had been somewhat rough edged—full of anarchy and murder and terrifying versions of love. *The Boatman's Call*, recorded after Cave divorced his first wife Viviane Carneiro and had a brief, intense affair with musician Polly Jean Harvey, is subdued. It harkens back to a sound the band hinted at on earlier ballads such as "The Ship Song," but with mostly just an organ and Cave's broken baritone, it was like nothing the band had ever recorded before. It remains one of their most critically acclaimed albums. Everyone can relate to mourning.

Before I leave for the Catskills, I ride the subway back and forth to work, listening to *The Boatman's Call* on earphones attached to my phone, weeping openly. That no one ever says anything to me on the train is one of the joys of New York City.

While I am gone, Tai and I start planning a reading series together from afar, for when I return to New York. While I am gone, Mya, who hasn't bothered to even attempt to write a breakup album about me, posts a song in a networking group I added her to months before. The song is called "I Don't Need You Anymore." It's pretty terrible and it's co-credited to a dentist who happens to make enough money to have a really great recording studio.

Bob Dylan has sworn up and down that *Blood on the Tracks* is not an autobiographical album, but rather an exercise based on Chekhov's stories. Most critics and fans feel that this is an obvious lie. Dylan's life as a musician is full of them—perhaps starting in the mid-sixties when he toyed with reporters endlessly instead of answering them outright. Most (including Dylan's son Jakob) feel that *Blood on the Tracks* is a chronicle of his love affair and divorce from his first wife and the mother of his children, Sara. I am firmly in the Dylan-is-a-liar autobiographical camp.

This album, re-recorded a few days before it was to go out into the world, is supplemented by the bootleg of the original version, often called *Blood on the Tapes*. The most significant difference, in my opinion, is that in the original version, the song "If You See Her, Say Hello" contains the line, "If you're makin' love to her, kiss her for The Kid." The Kid had been Joan Baez's nickname for Dylan years before, when they were involved. One heartbreak is all heartbreaks.

In a moment of what may have been candor, Dylan famously said of his breakup album, "A lot of people tell me they enjoyed that album. It's hard for me to relate to that—I mean, people enjoying that type of pain."

We don't exactly *enjoy* it. But there is something about the breakup album, something about knowing that heartbreak is universal. There is a section that I always return to in the Sherman Alexie story "What You Pawn, I Will Redeem." The story tells about the trials of a homeless Native American man who finds his dead grandmother's ceremonial regalia in a pawn shop and vows to get the money to buy it back. In one section of the story, he meets several Aleut fisherman waiting on the docks. He asks them if they can sing him some songs. They say that they know all of Hank Williams. He says, no, he wants the sacred songs. They say Hank Williams *is* sacred.

I think about these lines a lot. I think about how one thing we all do, no matter who we are, is feel heartbreak. It can be from lost love, or lost family, even lost pets. It can be from the end of marriage, or the end of a life. But we all mourn when the future we have assumed will always be there is suddenly gone. We all feel the emptiness of moments when someone we expected to be in them is not. Grief, when it hits you like a car crash, leaves you reeling and groping to find meaning and narrative to explain your loss. And that people have invented a musical equivalent of the process of loss sometimes feels like the most sacred thing in the world.

◇◇

When I get back into town, I try to meet up with the woman who I'd had a threesome with with Tai. She is excessively depressed. I take her to Washington Square Park and bring taramosalata and tapenade and all sorts of salty foods. We sit on a blanket and eat them as she talks about her sadness. All around us, the end of summer is hanging from the dark green tree leaves. The performers are busking under the granite arch, old folkies are singing songs they've been singing for decades. I want to be a life raft for her. I cannot. Enter that quote that people are always telling me about putting on your own mask first when the airplane starts going down.

◇◇

The first night that Tai and I spend together, alone, after both of us thinking the other would rather be dating the woman I used to work with, we go out to have beers with some literary douchebag that Tai doesn't like, but who they are using to get closer to the community they want to be part of. When a woman who is at our table leaves, the literary douchebag confides in Tai and me that he's slept with her. He doesn't say it because he wants advice on how to proceed. He just wants us to know.

Tai and I leave, and we talk shit on him for a while. He's an Ernest Hemingway want-to-be, he even looks like him. We like privately talking shit on other writers almost as much as we like each other. So-and-so has gender essentialist politics, even though they're trans. Someone-else writes for a shitty website and talks about it at parties like she's won a Pulitzer. We know we are supposed to give a shit about such-and-such's writing, but we just couldn't possibly care any less.

We kiss at the entrance to the subway. Tai is much taller than me, and they stoop down to kiss me as I get up on my toes. I invite them back to my apartment, where we spend the night in my bed. When we wake up early the next morning, we listen to the greatest love song ever, Tom Waits's "Jersey Girl." It's the greatest love song ever because no one would drive regularly from New York City to New Jersey to see someone unless they really loved them. And Tom Waits, who had before that sung about dishwater blonds in coffee shops, is still married to the woman he wrote it about forty years later. We don't listen to the Tom Waits version, though. We listen to the cover by the The Hell Blues Choir, sung in a halting, over-pronounced English-as-a-second-language lilt. The morning is gray, and I might be able to fall in love again, maybe.

◇◇

    I tell Tai stories while we are in my bed in Brooklyn. I tell them about how I got my bellybutton pierced in my hometown at age fifteen without parental consent because one of my friends (also fifteen) flashed the much-older piercer her breasts. I tell Tai about the time I walked into a show of Mya's she hadn't expected me to be at on Valentine's Day, and she was telling the story of violating my sexual boundaries as funny stage banter. I tell Tai about the time I took crystal meth three days before an international flight, not realizing it affected you for days on end, and ended up coughing up blood in a hostel in Europe, my suitcase filled with Mexican wrestling masks and pink beehive wigs.
    "Sometimes your stories scare me," they say, blinking at me.
    Tai and I make each other playlists on Spotify. They put the saddest Sun Kil Moon songs they can find on theirs. I put Jonathan Byrd's "Hazel Eyes" and Diana Jones' "My Remembrance of You" on mine. Tai is impressed by their obscurity. I end the playlist with some of my favorite breakup songs.

    I set up a reading event in Detroit, at an anarchist collective house and performance space. Tai offers to drive. We realize on the day we're supposed to leave that we can't get a car anywhere in New York with our debit cards, and begin to panic. We take a train out to JFK Airport at the far end of Queens, but the story there is the same. We try to get on a bus to Detroit, but the last one is already full. Tai calls a man they know from sex work, who they say loves them and will do anything for them. He doesn't do anything for us. Finally, the morning of the show, we find a sketchy rental place and procure a car with bad steering. We make it to Detroit just in time to drink a few glasses of Bulleit rye before going on stage.

The next day, I stay to explore the ruins of Detroit, which remind me so much of the town I grew up in, while Tai drives back alone. I buy a Greyhound ticket back to New York. Before Tai leaves, they tell me that if I'm going to keep touring for my book, they'll come with me, they'll drive me anywhere I want to go.

Tai and I become primary partners. We are going to move to Detroit and renovate an old house. We are going to buy dogs. We are going to adopt kids.

This happens in less than a month. Maybe you see where this is going.

Willie Nelson wrote *Phases and Stages*, a fictional breakup album that chronicled two sides of a breakup. Like Sinatra's *In the Wee Small Hours of the Morning*, it was revolutionary for its genre. No country singer had ever released a concept album before this one. While it can be argued that Willie Nelson transcends the genre of country at times, the album is firmly in that camp. Side one is dedicated to the woman's side of the story, and side two is dedicated to the man's.

While I admire this album (compulsive heterosexuality aside), can you ever tell two sides of things? Can I tell you how jealous Tai felt when I introduced them to another partner of mine and we kissed in greeting, like we always did? Can I tell you how Tai felt when they went away to a poetry reading in Canada with someone else they were dating, one I had wanted to go to but had been unable to, and the other person posted a picture of the two of them kissing on the internet, and I sent Tai a message, breaking up with them while they were stuck in a car with three other people? Can I tell you how embarrassed Tai felt that they'd been asking their uncles for advice on fixing up old houses for months, and I had broken it off with a text message? Can I tell you what was in their head as we kind of got back together, then they left me to move to Iowa with the other person? Can I tell you why Tai lied and told me, yeah, sure, of course they'd been in non-monogamous relationships before, when it absolutely was not true? Not really.

I can't even really tell you why, when it was over, I told Tai that our relationship had been a meaningless rebound to me when *that* was absolutely not true. Why would I do that other than that I was hurt and wanted to hurt in return? I regret this behavior. I always do.

"It's not supposed to be that way," Willie sings in *Phases and Stages*. "You're supposed to know that I love you."

I don't think Tai was able to deal with how sad I wanted to be.

◇◇

Once, shortly before Tai leaves me for someone who posts Pokemon pictures on their Facebook wall instead of boring them about breakup albums, we drunkenly get in an argument in the shower. I had been talking about how, when PJ Harvey and Nick Cave broke up, he'd talked endlessly in the media about how *The Boatman's Call* was about her. She had said something along the lines of the album she wrote after their break up, *Is This Desire?*, having the best sound she'd ever achieved in her career, and nothing else.

He was a footnote to her breakup album, I say, one that she never even mentioned by name. I talk about how amazing that is, how easy it would have been to make that her Nick Cave album when others insisted that's what it was. *Rolling Stone* tried to pin her song "Angelene" down as a response to Cave's call of "West Country Girl." But Harvey never played that game. She experimented with sound, some songs whisper and some songs wail; she experimented with narrative and came up with something that is hardly evocative of their relationship at all, but resonant with ends and heartbreak and disillusionment.

But Tai doesn't agree. They argue that no, *Harvey* was the footnote, she was reduced to the object of love instead of her role as formidable artist. We aren't really arguing. We are washing our own and each others' bodies, drunk, kissing under the hot water of the shower.

I never wrote the book on breakup albums. I wrote a listicle.

The last I heard of Tai, they moved back to Brooklyn from Iowa and married the person they left me for. They got accepted into one of the most prestigious Masters of Fine Arts programs in writing in the country. Did I ever bother to mention that Tai is one of the best poets I've ever met? I realize I've also never said that Tai would feed me tortillas fried in coconut oil and topped with homemade vegan sour cream and black beans when I was sad. That if Tai came over, and I cooked for them, they would do thoughtful things for me while I did, like change out the litter in my cat's box, or sweep my bedroom. That they have a ridiculous love of malt liquor and lurking in alleyways, drinking it. That they're brilliant about philosophy in ways that make my brain twist up. That they love Bolano and Perec, and when they read poetry with me they would check in with what I was reading first so they could read something to compliment it. How they'd look when I'd catch sight of their silhouette across the street when they'd come to my part of Brooklyn to see me at a diner at 3:00 a.m. About the night that I rode a train with them to Staten Island, where they were having electrolysis for hair removal, and I sat in a waiting room, late into the night, while they yelled in pain above the buzz of machinery in a room where I couldn't go and hold their hand. That they foster rescue cats, which they say comes with the understanding that it will always end in heartbreak for them, but a better life for their foster in the long run.

I never said these things because I never thought about them then. I thought more about books I was going to write and research I was going to do. I thought about the bright spot inside me I felt when they were around, when everything else had been so dark, a crack in a tunnel I was unsure had an end. But I never thought about them the way they deserved to be thought about. I never thought about them more than I thought about songs written by old sad men, and my own sadness.

Flowered Ties (Part One)

Mya and I are about six months into our marriage when Mya meets Vivien at the Trans Ladies' Picnic and they start dating. I don't go to the TLP (obviously; I'm not a trans lady), and I often find trans-masc spaces intimidating. I am not yet on testosterone; my still-scrawny androgyne body doesn't conform to ideas of masculinity; I have no plans for surgeries of any kind; I only wear my chest binder when I feel like it. I had tried once to go to a support group, and the trans-masc folks had made me feel so unwelcome, so un-"male-identified," that I'd left in tears. So most of the people who come to Mya's and my apartment are trans women.

Vivien still goes back and forth between using her old name and going to work at the Museum of Natural History dressed in her men's clothes, and dressing more comfortably and using her real name on weekends. She is quiet, and gentle, until she isn't— like the day some old man clandestinely takes pictures of me, her, and Mya on the subway, and she catches on, gets up, grabs his phone, erases the pictures, berates him, and throws the phone down the length of the subway while everyone on the train watches in terror.

After years of marriage, Vivien is new to non-monogamy, but is also the sole person who sleeps with my wife who asks about my boundaries and feelings—which, I would learn later, Mya was typically lax in discussing or, really, caring about. I am grateful for Vivien's care. We become close quite quickly. I'm compiling second-hand clothing for a new, more masculine wardrobe, and Vivien gives me several of the ties she no longer wears or wants. They are all bright, mostly pink. Some have stripes, some have flowers. They had always been, she says, her way of signaling that she was not quite as straight and cis as she appeared to the untrained eye.

One has small, pink daisies on it, the kind you'd draw precisely on a middle school notebook cover. She'd worn it to her wedding, she says. She and her now-in-the-process-of-becoming-ex-wife had been together since they were teenagers in Greenpoint, Brooklyn. They'd gotten married at a courthouse, then had their wedding reception at a diner in Long Island City. She didn't need it anymore, but she didn't want to just throw it away. I'd been married in a garden in the East Village, in a second-hand designer dress that I'd found at the Salvation Army, with sequins and cats stitched on it—it was better than that sounds. I understand.

The tie is too wide for my style, but I wear it anyway.

◇◇

That year, Mya and I host Halloween, Thanksgiving, Hanukkah, and Passover at our apartment, and Vivien always comes. Each time, Vivien thanks us the next day for welcoming her into our home, as if she isn't a part of it. She is. But also. We know that lots of us need a family we don't have otherwise.

That was the vision of non-monogamy I'd given to Mya when I first met her, when I'd explained to her that she didn't have to cheat on her partners, she just had to be honest. You could have so many people in life you loved, who you chose, who chose you, not who were bound to you by genetics or blood or law. Back in those early days, I'd filled her head with the thoughts that filled mine: any number of people who would be around to care, to raise children together, to be your true self for. This was the idea of family we all wanted, and many of us clung to with our lives.

One night, in the winter, Vivien's divorce is getting worse, her ex-wife is acting more and more cruelly, out of her own pain, and Vivien is missing her children more and more. She and Mya and I all snuggle up, fully clothed, in my and Mya's bed. It is Sunday, the early evening is dark. Vivien and I both have to go back to work the next day, to our office jobs that we don't like, but that we both need.

I play Leonard Cohen's first album while we are all lying there in the dark. Vivien has never heard it. It's so sad and haunting, winter through and through, his still-young, still-innocent voice carrying the poetry over hints of guitar. Mya and I listen as if we have never heard it before either. For an hour, no one says anything. We are all awake, listening, holding each other, our chins snuggled into each other's shoulder hollows.

Towards the end of the album, Mya gets up and turns the lights on. She is bored.

◇◇

Vivien moves in with another friend, after finally leaving her home, her wife, and her children. Sometimes she talks about the dog that she'd had since childhood, buried in the backyard of a home she is no longer welcome in.

She doesn't have a bed at her new home. She sleeps on the floor. I don't think she feels like she deserves a bed.

It is on the floor, in the dark, where Mya and I find her, one day, when we stop by to make sure she is okay. She has an empty bottle of cheap vodka beside her, and a plastic bag that she's been trying in vain to seal around her neck. She is crying. Her kids, she misses them so much.

In that moment Mya is perfect, holding Vivien and promising her it will be okay.

◇◇

When Mya had surgery on her vocal chords a few years before the day we found Vivien, I'd given her a teddy bear to take to the hospital with her. His name was Little Bear. I hadn't know this then, but Mya's mother had once told her that she would know she'd found the love of her life when she found her teddy bear. I think maybe the way this played out was not what her mother had in mind.

The day we find Vivien on the floor, Mya and I take her to our house and give her one of my old teddy bears. We name her after Leonard Cohen's "Suzanne."

Vivien and Mya and I all go to the vacation house of a trans guy we've recently met. We drive for hours, Mya behind the wheel, and Vivien and I getting drunk on cheap wine in the car.

The situation at the vacation house is somewhat uncomfortable—the guy just hired his new girlfriend in the business he runs, and introduces all of us as part of the family that surrounds this business. The new girlfriend is great; we kind of question him, though. We have known him less than two months at this point. There are other people there who have known him longer, and no one raises an eyebrow.

There is a hot tub at the vacation house with multi-colored lights, and we all climb in it. Vivien goes inside the house, comes back out, goes inside and comes back out. Finally, she takes off her clothes and gets into the hot tub and sits uncomfortably for a while. Someone laughs at my orange sports bra and camouflage boxer-briefs—am I going hunting? I take it with better nature that I usually do teasing from strangers. We are all trans, and all our bodies are configurations of what is generally considered "normal." A little teasing about my attire seems trivial in comparison to the freedom to be nearly-naked and not have pieces of my body come into question.

Months later, Vivien will get up on a stage and tell the story of struggling to reveal her trans body to a half dozen other trans bodies. She will tell how doing so made her hide in a bed tucked into a nook for the rest of the weekend. She will tell how Mya would always praise her for being so tough, so badass, and how, in the moment she takes off her clothes, she will wonder if she could be anything further from those things.

While she is on the stage, telling her story, she will take off all her clothes and reveal her trans body to a hundred people.

Vivien ends up in a hospital. The few days before she is admitted, when she is just back from helping a friend recover from surgery in Thailand, she spends at Mya's and my apartment. She and Mya and I go to the grocery store, and Vivien is obviously not doing well. She keeps poking at and moving fish heads in the refrigerated meats aisle. Mya gets angry with her, tells her to stop it. Vivien says she is trying to reassemble them.

When Vivien is diagnosed, Mya uses her diagnosis to break up with her, saying she'd been abused by someone with a similar diagnosis and couldn't handle it.

That day, the day of the fish heads, before the hospital,

Vivien makes us the most amazing mushroom soup from scratch. She misses cooking for her family, she says.

◇◇

When Mya leaves me, when I am alone in our apartment, when my last hopes for a life with family and community seem to have vanished, I talk to Vivien on Facebook chat while I google the most painless ways to commit suicide. I stumble around the internet until I find a method that involves using an "exit bag." An exit bag is a plastic bag filled with helium or some other gas that prevents panic when attempting to die by substituting it for oxygen.

I remember one day when Mya, my friend Jad, and I had gone for a walk in Queens, along the East River, in Astoria Park. Under the overpass where cars and trains rattled, there had been a high concrete wall with a guardrail. At the base of the wall was a tiny strip of beach. The beach was heaped with sea glass. The gentle waves of the river washed more up on the sand; it brushed against the sea glass on the shore and made the sound of windchimes between the roars of passing cars. This, I decided, was where I would like to die. I told Vivien. She threatened to call the police, but I made her promise she wouldn't, with the logic that I was a mentally ill trans person and could end up dead from an encounter with the cops, and then she'd have to live with that. I told her I was only telling her so that she wouldn't worry if I was missing.

◇◇

It's fairly common, among people like us, to trade clothes. There are many in-person and online clothing exchanges for transgender folks. In fact, it's one of the leading ways, in early transition, that we shed who we were and become someone new. It seems particularly resonant that we often do it as a community, with the people our friends once were a major part of the people we are becoming.

When I wear ties, I almost exclusively wear skinny ties. I have a few that once belonged to Mya's grandfather that I adore, silk relics from the '70s. But, hanging in my closet, are still many ties that I rarely wear, that once signaled to the world who Vivien was, underneath who she felt she had to be.

Home in Three Meals

1.

I want to teach writing and storytelling classes at the shelter for homeless LGBTQ+ kids under 23. I want to do it, but the volunteer director takes a look at my resume, at my bookstore office job, at my Salvation Army clothes, and he asks me if I would like to cook for the residents once a week instead. The perfectly dressed girl in my orientation who works for the ACLU is asked if she would like to be a life mentor for the residents.

Okay, I think. *I'm happy to go where they need me.* But it still hurts.

A few weeks later, I find myself standing at the bus stop, waiting to cross Queens to the shelter. The documentary *The Dog* has just been released, and as I stand in front of the poster for it, I take a selfie of me in John Wojtowicz's silhouette and text it to Mya. *The Dog* is the true story behind the film *Dog Day Afternoon*, in which a man robs a bank to pay for his suicidally depressed trans lover's operation.

Mya and I are newly married, living in an apartment in the Astoria neighborhood. She asks me if I am planning to rob a bank. She tells me she'll have dinner ready for me when I get home. The bus arrives.

I get to the church basement kitchen. There are no instructions. There are no sharp knives. There is a key to a freezer full of meat and vegetables, a bag of potatoes, and a few boxes of Rice-a-roni.

I am very, very poor when I live in Queens. $1200 income a month poor, when my rent excluding bills is $700. I make it work. I guess I am not the greatest role model, though.

My wife and I love each other, I think at the time, and we are having fun, being artists, running from one event to the next across New York, and transitioning genders together. I have become stagnant on activism since I graduated from college, and I want to give something back, even though I don't have anything really to give. Time, I have time. I will give that.

Cooking for thirty kids is a challenge. First of all, there are the logistics of it. There is a small oven, a stovetop, and a toaster oven. There is just barely enough space to time thirty meals at the same time, and you can't exactly have half of the kids eat and half of the kids wait. Then, there is the fact that they are kids, and kids have notoriously shitty palates. I try to think of what I ate as a kid. Eventually, I begin making cheese sauces to pour over the boiled broccoli they leave uneaten on their plates.

What's that? One of the kids asks the first time she sees the orange mixture bubbling in the saucepan.

Cheese sauce. For your vegetables.

No one's ever done that before, she says.

No one....ever made you cheese sauce so you'd eat your vegetables?

No, she says.

It will be a sentiment I will hear repeated often—when I make them shepherd's pies on cold winter nights, when I make them real mashed potatoes instead of boxed ones. When I offer to make pie crust for two large pot pies, the counselor in charge of the shelter looks at me with something like confusion. *Isn't that difficult?* he asks.

The fire alarm in the basement is so hair-triggered that steam from a boiling pot of water can set it off. I spend half of my time waving pot holders at it, trying to make it stop beeping incessantly. Half of the time I wonder if everything is horrible, burning. Once in a while, things do burn, and I feel horrible.

The residents in the shelter don't seem to mind. They chat about their dreams, the drama going on at any given moment in the residence, their ideal future houses—will it be a rich apartment in Manhattan, or a shady place out in the boroughs where no one will mind that all their friends are addicts and sex workers? Occasionally they'll disclose details of being thrown out of their homes, which mostly revolve around parents who couldn't deal with their children being queer.

I haven't spoken to my own family in years at that point. My wife, the community of queer people I move in, the friends

I have collected over the years are my only family. They are where all my own dreams reside. I don't have anything to say to make any of it better.

◇◇

One day, I remember what my grandmother fed me for practically half of the meals I ate as a child. Homemade, hand-cut french fries. They were my favorite. They were the favorite of all her grandchildren. She passed away long ago. I can still remember dipping oil-hot fries into ketchup to cool them down enough to take a bite, because I couldn't wait.

There happens to be a bag of potatoes and some hamburger patties at the shelter. I decide to give burgers and hand-cut fries a try.

The first batch of potatoes I cut into fries with a butter knife comes out a soggy, oily mess. Not fries. Then I remember my grandmother telling me that the first batch always came out the worst, that you needed to let the oil get very, very hot. I try again, and the fries begin to brown and crisp. I fry up pan after pan.

The residents start taking plates. A girl with her arm in a cast comes up to me and says, Can I have some more french fries? I cut and fry potatoes until the entire bag is gone.

Riding the bus home, with the smell of oil clinging to me and my grandmother's love wrapped around me as it hasn't been since she died 15 years before, I cry.

2.

Mya runs off to San Francisco with another trans girl who she says truly understands her. It doesn't matter that the girl breaks up with her a month later for being "too clingy." My life has been destroyed.

I take a job as a pastry cook at a resort on a mountaintop. A chef teaches me how to make cheesecakes, molten cakes, meringues, rum-infused whipped creams, doughnuts, fruit compotes, marshmallows, cookies, scones. I dive into baking as a kind of therapy. It is not like other forms of cooking. It is sweet and frivolous, something you can live without. Baked goods exist for the sole purpose of happiness.

I spend all summer on that mountain top, writing, baking, hiking down paths green with the sunlight that shines through the leaves of trees. I begin to dream of things I might do. I will learn everything I can about pastry cooking. I will open a queer-themed bakery called Coming Out Cupcakes with items named after famous gay people. It will run as a non-profit, teaching trans people who can't find other employment all the skills that have been given to me.

I apply for a non-profit fellowship in Detroit, citing that my ultimate goal is to open this jobs training program. I said my reason for wanting to open it there is the large number of trans folks involved in sex work who have been murdered in the city in the same park, because they have no other options. Unsurprisingly, they also don't look upon me as a great role model, or fit for the program. I don't give up on the idea, though.

One day, about two years into my quest to learn everything I can about pastry cooking, I am working mornings as a pastry cook and bread baker, and nights as a server. A table is unhappy with their meal, unhappy with their drinks, defiant of any attempts to please them. As an attempt to save their experience, I buy them dessert—a disc of lemon chiboust resting in a pool of blackberry compote. I've made it myself, I promise them it is light, airy, mostly meringue, but brightened by the fruits and their interplay. They eat each bite with smiles on their faces.

Desserts make people happy. I don't really care for sweets myself, but I want to do something that is just for the purpose of goodness and nothing else.

3.

I am living in my first solo apartment in rural Ohio. It is way too big for me and my cat; I constantly think about ways I can move someone else in. Perhaps a refugee family, for a short time. Maybe a friend's friend who is escaping domestic abuse.

I quit baking professionally. With the affordable care act threatening to disappear, I am worried I can't sustain myself in the restaurant industry any longer. I am thinking of taking a job in car insurance. I have passed all their tests, and they tell me they think they can use my empathy for their claims department. It seems like hell. But I am trying to figure out how I can take care of myself. I am trying to figure out how I can move on with my life, buy a house, adopt a kid alone.

I am still broke. Eating isn't always easy. I start freelance writing, and things get a little better. I think maybe I will do some food writing, but all I have to say about food is stories of vegan holiday meals I cooked with my queer family in New York. I feel too unsure about baking to say anything with authority.

A friend writes an essay about a traditional Indian dish her grandmother taught her how to make to help heal her of her first broken heart. I think of all the foods my grandmother cooked for me when I was a child. The most special one I can think of is white borscht.

It wasn't special because it was a huge delicacy or anything like that. It was special because she made it once a year, on Easter. It contained all the elements of a traditional Polish Catholic blessed Easter basket. The egg representing rebirth, the horseradish representing the bitter tears of Christ, and so on. I don't believe in any of that stuff, but I do miss my grandmother's Easter borscht. When I'd been in my early 20s and living in Greenpoint, Brooklyn, the old Polish women rushing to have their baskets blessed on Easter Saturday had reminded me so much of her. I'd tracked down every restaurant that had served white borscht in the area and sampled all of them. None were quite like my grandmother's.

The year before, when my cousin's daughter, Jessica, died far too young, my twenty-two year old niece called me to talk. She had grown up with this cousin, visiting her in Pennsylvania every few years. She was distraught. I told her about how Jessica's Uncle Jason, my cousin, had died when I was her age. All I remember of those days is the small, mean town we lived in and all the drugs all of us took. Some of us got out alive and some of us did not. The last thing my niece could remember our cousin Jessica saying to her was how lucky she was that she had grown up in Los Angeles, and not in Wilkes-Barre, where all the problems were growing.

That day, my niece said that she was happy she still had me. That I was her only link to that part of her family that she had left. She was mine, too. She told me that she was going to attempt to make our grandmother's white borscht the night she learned that our cousin had died.

I've done a lot of cooking in my life, but I've never tried to make my grandmother's borscht. There is one step I can never remember. I read my friend's article on the food her grandmother cooked to heal her heart, and I begin looking up recipes for white borscht.

What I remembered is this—you boil kielbasa in water, and reserve the water. You add vinegar and something else—egg perhaps?—to thicken it. Then, when it is thickened, you warm it and add sliced hardboiled egg, sliced kielbasa, ham, pork butt, and horseradish. But what is that missing step?

When I tell my niece I am trying to cook borscht, she sends me the recipe she has been using. It turns out that the missing step is that you thicken sour cream with flour. Then, you pour a bit of the vinegar and kielbasa water into the sour cream and flour mixture to warm it up. Then you whisk the whole thing back into the boiling water.

That's my favorite part! My niece says to me, via Skype. *It's quite satisfying.*

It's almost just like "proofing" eggs, I say, *when you make a custard. Which is my favorite part of pastry cooking.*

It's a delicate process, but easy once you get the hang of it. If it's done wrong, things curdle. If you do it just right, simultaneously whisking and adding warm to cold, it comes out smooth and resilient to hot temperatures.

Sitting alone in my first solo apartment, I taste the soup my grandmother made once a year, which I have not tasted since I was 14. It is just like hers. I can't believe that it has taken me this long to think I could make it myself, any time I want, any time I think of her.

Psychopomps

It is important to note, however, that deities associated with such traits did not preside over gendered or sexual behavior or identity merely, but that they also functioned in other capacities, serving as creators, guardians, healers, peacemakers, psychopomps (guides of souls from one world to the next) and still other capacities.
—Queer Myth, Symbol, and Spirit

Vivien showed up to read her poetry in a gold-sequined dress the night that she saved the life of a teenage trans girl who posted a suicide note onto a large Facebook group. She wore her round, movie star sunglasses even though it was nighttime. I knew Vivien before, just before, she became who she is. Her clothes then were baggy, non-descript, as if she were trying to disappear into them. She used to occasionally wear pink ties with flowers and bold, bright designs.

We were in a shabby house in a very expensive part of Brooklyn. The carpets were threadbare and the door didn't quite close unless the deadbolt was in place. A million people lived there, and they all ran the art series Vivien was reading at. There were people there from the local queer press, the usual trans poetry scene folks. The people who ran the series were musicians who were socially conscious. They liked to provide a platform for people like us. We take our opportunities where we can.

I came into the house and found Vivien in the bathroom, putting on glitter. She didn't care about the things that used to bother her anymore, like her hairline which she had once hidden with bandanas. She looked beautiful. She was shining, literally. I hugged her.

I walked back out to the kitchen where a woman named Nina was sitting. I knew her by reputation, it was hard not to with some folks. I'd heard story after story about her in the past— she had sex in the back of someone's car while the person was driving, she liked to send unsolicited nude photos to people. The person I saw sitting in front of me didn't seem like she was the same person I'd heard about. She seemed awkward and shy. I struck up a conversation with her. Was she a writer, too? I asked.

"I guess I wouldn't call myself that," she said, and looked down at her beer.

The show started. Vivien read third. Before her set began, sitting on the floor of the living room in the audience as she was being introduced, I raised my voice to the audience, "Vivien also traced a photo to track down the address of a teenage trans girl who'd swallowed a bunch of sleeping pills in the UK this morning. The girl's okay and Viv saved her life."

Everyone clapped and Vivien blushed under her glitter

makeup shimmer. The minute I'd seen the suicide note posted on the Facebook group, I knew she would not only be able to find the girl because of her skills with doxxing people online, but that she would be invested in making sure the girl survived. And she had helped, immediately and without question.

"Hocray, Saint Vivien!" yelled one of the women who ran the queer press.

Vivien read her poetry. A few queer superstar writers showed up after the show was over, and a seventeen-year-old girl from New Jersey named Elana threw up in the bushes on the side of the house where the neighborhood cats hid. Later, Elana would tell me it was the best night of her life.

Vivien was angry. There was any number of things that would make her fly into a rage. We argued all the time, and the really frustrating thing was that most of the time she was right. Being friends with someone with great morals is obnoxious.

Vivien had her limits, though. She often didn't have much empathy to offer people outside her community. When I got to her apartment that day, she was furious over some relative of a friend who had asked a trans person on the internet if they were a "true hermaphrodite."

"A fucking hermaphrodite," Vivien raged. "As if we were in the '50s."

"Do you know the story of Hermaphroditus?" I asked.

"Son of Hermes and Aphrodite—Hermes the guide to the underworld and Aphrodite the goddess of love. So their child would, I guess, be the one who holds your hand with compassion when you die, eases you out of life, if god genealogy works like that, which I don't think it does. Anyway—this nymph fell in love with him, and prayed to the gods that they would be together always, but the gods pulled a Monkey's Paw on her and combined her and Hermaphroditus so that she disappeared completely and Hermaphroditus became this blend of who the two had been."

"Why are you telling me this?" Vivien said. She was still angry, but calming down.

"I don't know. The word goes back pretty far, past the '50s. Writing something about him, I guess."

Vivien sighed. "Yeah. Sometimes I wish I believed in things. Anything, really."

She didn't, though, not as far as I knew her. The things she did, the good things—they were just for the world as it was, not for some future heaven or far away utopia.

The girl from the UK had gotten out of the hospital she'd been sent to after Vivien doxxed her. Vivien spent a lot of time talking to her on the internet. She corrected her gently when she made bad jokes about weight or looks or poverty. The girl was a snot nose, really, a total brat wrapped up in her own beauty and the men who were constantly offering to marry her. Vivien didn't care. Vivien was patient.

◇◇

Elana was a really good kid. She got mad, though, if you ever told her that.

"I'm not a kid," she'd say. "I took care of my crazy mother all through my childhood. I grew up fast."

Whenever Vivien called her "kiddo," whenever my roommate tried to convince her that maybe dating Nina, who was 20 years older than her, was not the best of ideas, she would come back with the same logic: she wasn't a kid and we shouldn't treat her like one.

Which, of course, was a very seventeen-year-old thing to say. We all loved Elana, though, watching and supporting as best we could as she spent all her time bouncing around from one inflatable mattress on a living room floor to another, all so she could stay in New York, so she could be in proximity to all the things she wanted—art and music and poetry and community and, of course, her growing relationship with Nina. None of us wanted to say it, but she gave us all a little hope. She knew who she was so young, so much younger than any of us ever had.

Nina called herself Elana's "trans mom" in public, saying she was teaching her how to be the woman she wanted to be. Sometimes, when Elana talked about their relationship, she sounded really uncomfortable.

You try telling a seventeen-year-old anything.

◇◇

Vivien was the only trans person I knew who had kids. Most of us had never wanted them, or had ended up unable to have them from hormone replacement therapy. Her kids had dealt with a lot, from their parents divorce to their dad becoming their second mom. They had a lot of support, but they grappled, anyway. I was always pretty sure they'd pull through fine.

One day I was at Vivien's house, with her and her roommate and her partner and her kids. Vivien's partner, Jams, was always calm, quiet, sometimes playing piano softly in the corner of the small kitchen/living room space. Vivien's kids played video games, ran around. Vivien loved cooking for them on the weekends she had them.

I was sitting on the couch reading while soft classical music drifted between the pops of the oil heating in a saucepan. Vivien's daughter had come in to pet the cat. Occasionally, I'd call out a bit of information from the book I had in front of me.

"Did you know that, of the ones that didn't just hang themselves outright after colonization, many Native American cultures' two-spirit people went underground? They either hid who they were completely, living as their assigned gender, or just went stealth, never acknowledging that they were ever any gender than the one they presented as. They kind of Trojan-horsed the tradition into the present, despite colonizers trying to eradicate it completely. Two-spirit people were traditionally considered a really valuable part of society, blessed and spiritually marked as special. Two-spirits were thought to have a unique view on the world that not many people shared."

"What do you know about Native American traditions?" Vivien said.

"Me? Nothing but what I'm reading."

Vivien's daughter looked around the room. The kid was six, going on seven. She had round cheeks, long blond hair, a little round belly and elbow dimples. She was adorable. She picked up the cat.

"Everyone has a gender friend!" she announced.

We all looked at her, and Vivien asked what she meant.

Vivien's daughter pointed to me and Jams. "You both used to be girls, but aren't anymore." She pointed at Vivien and her roommate, Fiona. "You both used to be boys, but now you're girls." She squeezed the cat. "Me and the cat are both girls, and we like being girls. We all have a gender friend."

It was kind of the most adorable thing ever, and I put my book down and hugged her. Vivien shook her head and said, "These kids are going to have such good stories to tell when they grow up."

"It'll all be normal by then," I said. "Things will come back around."

"I don't think so," Vivien said. "I hope so. But I don't think so."

Vivien was sitting on the floor, in a circle of people, in a different run-down house in a different part of Brooklyn that was also very expensive. She was reading a poem about Sundays, the day after her kids went back home, and she was left with nothing but quiet. The welling tears in her eyes were ruining her glitter makeup.

◇◇

    The girl from the UK posted pictures of herself in fur coats that men bought her. She was beautiful, really. I remembered her suicide note, where she said she couldn't stand how ugly she was, she couldn't stand the thought that she would never walk down the street and have people see her the way she saw herself. Now, sometimes, she posted about how sorry she felt for ugly trans people that would never pass. Vivien reminded her that not everyone's goal was to pass.

    Elana would come over, needing a couch to sleep on, and I would let her drink one of my beers, but not more than one. She had been really bright-eyed, full of wonder, when I'd met her. She was growing increasingly sad, bitter. She still talked about all the art she loved, sometimes. But mostly she talked about Nina, who she was pulling away from, who she was so confused and hurt by. She talked about all the people around Nina, who she no longer held in such high regard. Maybe things weren't quite right after all.

    I read about Saint Perpetua, who dreamed she turned into a man to fight a lion in an amphitheatre. Of course the lion wasn't a lion. The lion was the Devil, also transformed.

When Perpetua was taken to the amphitheatre in real life, to be torn apart by beasts, they wouldn't touch her. And, so, she was stabbed to death.

◇◇

I read about the god of death, who made mermaids sing and fireflies flash a path for the boy in the moon to follow to him, taking him as his queer lover for times longer than man's. The boy in the moon was just a boy, nonetheless.

◇◇

Nina started reading in the shabby houses in Brooklyn. New worlds, cyborg trans women, witches, the fantastical. Everyone applauded.

◇◇

I kept trying to work the sacred mythologies from the far past, from trans history, into my stories, somehow. I kept failing. There was always a missing link, something damaged and broken irreparably, that I couldn't ever express. We had been one thing, once. We were now something quite other than that.

One day, in the last days before Elana left for college out West, she posted on Facebook exactly what had happened with Nina. The sex she felt pressured into. The insistence that things she did not want would be good in developing her into the person she wanted to be. Nina was in the middle of running a pretty high-profile workshop for a queer press. Many people ran to Nina's defense. She was a leader, and leaders were always attacked, they said. Elena felt alone. Isolated. She was nineteen, by then.

Vivien tried to preside over an accountability process with Nina, which fell apart. Nina wouldn't be held accountable for anything, other than to admit she, like everyone else, had flaws.

One day, the Facebook page of the girl from the UK went dead silent. For months, Vivien kept posting on it.
You still here?
Where are you?
There was no answer.

Flowered Ties (Part Two)

After my divorce, I am able to move back to New York after a summer away in the Catskills because of the kindness of community. My old roommate, a cis-het woman who moved her boyfriend in and changed the locks while I was gone, citing my divorce as traumatic for her, does not count among that community.

Vivien, who is now living with her partner Jams, her friend Fiona, and any assortment of homeless trans people, lets me sleep on the fold-out they have in the living room. I stay on their couch for weeks, while my cat stays at my partner Oscar's house and clearly hates me for abandoning her. I am habitually unable to find a roommate that will take both me and my ill-mannered rescue cat. I cannot find a place that will take just me and my cat without the promise of a ludicrous multiple of the rent in the income of the guarantor. I don't have any such thing.

Sometimes, when I am sitting on the couch in Vivien's living room, I talk casually about overdosing on my psychotropic medications. I make Vivien promise she will take care of my cat, who I am sure will live longer than me. Vivien sits next to me and googles all the horrible things that will happen to my body before I die if I overdose on these pills, relating them to me in a neutral voice.

Eventually, a woman named Jessie lets me move into the apartment she has just bought in Sunset Park. She lets me pay less than the room is worth, because she knows I am working in a kitchen and can't afford more. The kindness makes my heart break. I never know what to do with kindness extended. She pretends flawlessly that she doesn't care when my asshole cat tears apart her brand new rug instead of the scratching post I kept trying to get her to use, saying, "The rug can take it." Even my suspecting she might have cared is more on me than Jessie.

When I am hesitant, when I ask if she minds if I have people over, when I hedge about roommate things, Jessie keeps telling me, "It's your apartment, too. You live here."

I never really believe her, though I know she is entirely sincere.

◇◇

The list of things I move into the apartment I share with Jessie are as follows:
- The bed I bought with Mya, new, even though I had never had a new bed once in my life.
- Sylvia, my cat.
- A suitcase full of baking books I stole from the common area in the resort I worked at the previous summer.

- Two copies of a newspaper from my hometown that did a feature on my first novel.
- The banjo my ex-wife gave to me the day we got married.
- My knives and pastry tools.
- Two suitcases full of second-hand clothes, including Vivien's old ties.

The meager amount of things I own, but do not bring, I keep in storage. They include a bed frame, a guitar, a bookcase, all eight boxes of my books, antique typewriters, a framed art print given to me by an old lover that shows a person with breasts and a purple strap-on sticking out of their underwear, and several boxes of old manuscripts and copies of short stories. I don't think I'll be staying long enough to need them.

I work in one of the top Zagat-rated restaurants in New York City. It isn't that I am that good—there is a shortage of people in NYC who can work for kitchen wages. I decided to live off of the money I'd saved while living for free at the resort upstate in the Catskills so I can learn more. My second-hand clothes don't matter. I wear a uniform at work, a chef's coat and pants, multiples of which the laundry folks who work there provide me with every Monday.

Tai and I fall in love around this time, even though it doesn't last. On New Year's Eve, I drink champagne and explode bursts of edible silver glitter onto black-cocoa glazed mousse at work, then come home to Tai hiding out in my room while Jessie has a party in the living room. They are just back from the second part of their gender affirming surgery in California. We exchange holiday gifts—I give them a fancy pen and a pocket notebook. I learn later that they write exclusively on their phone. They give me a copy of Bolano's *Tres*. I've never read it, though I still have it.

◇◇

I do a storytelling event that November. Mya, who I've been speaking with again, and who is in the city briefly, comes to it with one of her new, radical, art-squat friends from Oakland. Later, she will tell me that she nudged her friend and told her, "See? I married them for a reason." As if the approval of these women is something I am seeking. As if I am her.

We have sex that night for the last time ever, in her mom's car, outside Vivien's house, where I am still staying. I have my period, even though I've recently begun taking testosterone. It's helping. I cry less already. I get blood on the center console of the car. Sometimes reality loops around more than fiction could ever remind itself to.

After, we go out for ice cream. When I tell Vivien and Jams and Fiona what happened, Fiona says, "Ah. A series of mistakes punctuated by one of life's greatest joys. Ice cream."

Months later, Mya will be back in town. It will be the last time we will see each other. We will have drinks at a bar down the street from the apartment I live in with Jessie. When she walks me home and asks to come inside to see our cat, I will tell her, no, she is not welcome.

I start dating a guy named Adam, who is cis, mostly het, and who works in tech. We will eventually joke a lot about how I made him gay. The joke is, that because I'm non-binary, everyone who sleeps with me is a little gay.

On our first date, in a brunch place near where we both live that I totally can't afford, I talk about the New York I loved in the early 2000s, the art loft I lived in in Bushwick where my share of the rent was $300 a month, the little cafes that catered to artists that don't exist anymore. He nods. It is his fault, he says, and the fault of folks like him. I shrug and tell him there are a great many people who see it as my fault, and I describe my then-unknowing role as a shock-wave gentrifier, an artist who is white and queer.

I am not trying to shame him. I actually like him a lot.

◇◇

Months later, after I am gone from the city and living a different life, Vivien will have a trans girl sleeping on her couch who can't get a foothold in New York. She will need bus fare back to her hometown that nobody can afford to give her.

Vivien will ask that I ask Adam for it. Adam can generally

be counted upon to help, but, honestly, I don't want anyone taking advantage of someone I, by then, care about a lot. I am careful to never take advantage of his generosity myself, no matter how many times he offers it. Vivien will get sort of angry with me when I hedge on asking him, and tell me I've forgotten completely where I came from myself.

Adam will not hesitate to buy the girl a bus ticket.

◇◇

Vivien's ties hang in my closet the whole time I live with Jessie. One night, I almost wear one to a party, but change out of it at the last minute.

◇◇

My money has almost run out. Tai is gone. I start making plans to leave New York. I tell Jessie, who understands, and begins to look for a new roommate. I tell Adam, who offers to give me part of his income so I can stay. There is no way I am taking it. I have been poor too long to not be proud.

◇◇

By the time Tai and I break up, in the spring, a lot of my things that were in storage are at their house. When we finally stop speaking for good, I try to rescue what I can. I sit there forlornly at the bus stop holding a suitcase full of unpublished short stories, old letters, and a framed art print with a person with breasts and a purple dick sticking out of their underwear.

◇◇

Later, after I have moved to Ohio, when Adam comes to visit and we stay in a hotel at Lake Erie, I decide I might love him.

Adam and I are sitting in the front seat of my car in a parking lot of a state park's beach in our bathing suits when I tell him how much comfort his non-normative body brings me in my non-normative body.

The first time we had sex, he paused in kissing me in the dark of his Brooklyn bedroom, still fully clothed, to mention that he had an ostomy pouch attached to his stomach. It was the curative measure for the Crohn's disease that had plagued him for years before I knew him, had sculpted the too-thin frame in pictures where he tried vainly to be silly but just looked so very ill.

"I'll be gentle," I promised.

"You don't have to be particularly gentle," he said, almost stammering. He was such an adorable nerd; I'd had to flat out say a few minutes before that I would rather kiss him than watch another episode of *MythBusters* with him.

"Well, while we're talking about things," I said. It was the perfect segue into the conversations I have to have about my body before sex. I began to describe the changes that had happened because of the testosterone I'd started taking a few months before, how my body might not be like the bodies he had seen or touched previously.

◇◇

A year later, in Ohio, we are staying in a motel in a small town on the lake that is horrible in a way I find delightful. I daydream about moving for the winter into a teal one-story motel with a pool that advertises color TV as one of its amenities, and writing stories about the other residents. I continue talking about bodies. Body hair is the thing that people usually peg as the first way my body is non-normative. As I sit there in my bathing suit—an outfit cobbled together after years of discomfort with male and female bathing suits, which consisted of a pair of black board shorts and a black rash guard surf t-shirt—I know the thing that people will stare at will by my thick, black leg hair. I went on about how it makes me feel less an object, and less alone, to know that there is someone standing next to me who also absorbs, in a completely different way, some of the gaze that focuses on the non-normative. Not a shield or a deflector. Simply someone who understands that the looks in eyes are there.

No one has ever suggested to Adam that he should have died instead of change his body to outmaneuver his illness, nor have I yet woken up in a hospital between doses of pain medication, my body cut into and knitting itself whole again. Our experiences don't match one-to-one. But somehow Adam also has gathered from his experiences in life the kindness to check out all the bathrooms in a bar to tell me which might be the safest or closest to my preferences, or to prep his friends before a social occasion on my correct pronouns, so the burden won't be completely on me.

Sitting in the front seat of my car, putting on my dark glasses, gathering our beach gear, I prepare myself mentally, and Adam pulls the waistband of his bathing suit up so only the top of his ostomy pouch was visible.

So, I might love him. We go to a pub crawl and have silly fun; he meets my oldest friend, who loves him; he lets her daughter use him as a diving board in her swimming pool; he is kind, funny, light-hearted, and generous, and a pain in the ass in his own unique way that I find charming. What isn't to love? Adam, to his credit, told me from day one that he was not into hierarchical non-monogamy, that he had no intentions of having a primary partner, and that he would never fall in love with anyone or marry them. So when he goes back to New York and I start thinking of him when I hear my favorite love songs, I decide to break up with him.

We talk it through. It is okay to love someone who doesn't love me back, I decide, as long as I don't let it take over my heart. We have since maintained a really lovely partnership, even though it has never eclipsed my common sense. Most likely because of that.

◇◇

When I decide to leave New York, I know I will never come back. I will never have the money to put a down payment on an apartment. I will never have the guarantor who can do it for me. I am the Wizard of Oz, shouting from the balloon that rises into the air, "I can't come back, I don't know how it works!"

I start giving away all my things. I am planning on going to Ohio with my cat and a suitcase, all I will be able to carry on the Amtrak train. Well, at least I will get some writing done on the way to Cleveland.

My books go to a small community bookstore in Crown Heights that let me host a reading series at it. My first-ever new mattress ends up on the curb. My guitar with the crack in its body and the sticker that says "I <3 Class Warfare" goes to Vivien's partner, Jams. Jams takes my wedding dress, too, after no one on Queer Exchange shows up to pick it up.

I hand Vivien back her wedding tie, though I keep the others. I never wear it anymore, I say. I don't want it to end up in the Salvation Army.

I also give Vivien a bracelet I wore at my wedding. My best friend gave it to me after she drove from Ohio with her husband and child to deliver a blessing. I can't wear it; I can't throw it away.

It is a wavy band with sparkling stones that slips over the wrist. Vivien's hands are smaller than mine, and it slides over them and onto her wrist, where it shimmers like the sequins she often wears.

Sometimes, these things, as little as they seem, are enough.

Genealogy (Part Two): Syncretism

Catholic saint stories are ghost stories, in a way. Tales of bodies disappearing, of miraculous events, of the blending of life and death, of the tearing of veils. I read a lot of saint stories in my '20s. I was an agnostic bordering on becoming an atheist. I kept asking of the texts, of the saints, of the ghosts, "Is this supposed to be real?"

Catholics put special meaning in the relics of saints. Catholicism is allegedly a monotheistic religion where it is okay to revere the knucklebone, or some other artifact, of someone blessed by God. Years after abandoning Catholicism, I would date someone whose religion was Santeria. He would talk to me about how, in his religion, Catholic saints stood in for Yoruban gods tramped down by Christianity and colonialism. It would mean a lot to me, how easily transferable one beloved entity was for another.

◇◇

My family believes in saints, and in ghosts. We are named after saints: my mother after Saint Barbara, my dad's mother Assunta after the Italian for Mary's ascension into Heaven. As a Catholic ritual, we choose our own middle names, after saints, in hopes they will protect us, in hopes they will strengthen our faith. My family also believes that the ones who matter to them will never leave. And so, our dead become our revered, and those who we can no longer reach reach for us through scrambled veils.

A patron saint is a guide. They can belong to a city, a person, a family, a profession, or an illness. My family name, DiFrancesco, carries the patron saint Francis of Assisi.

The night my father's mother Assunta falls down the stairs carrying a vacuum cleaner up them and is hospitalized, my father predicts her death.

He wakes up in the night. He and my mother still share the same bed—it is before I am born. He reaches for her, wakes her, tells of her a dream in which his mother died.

The phone rings.

◇◇

Once, when I was very ill, before I stopped speaking to my family, before I came out as transgender, I sat on the swing on the back porch of my family home with my mom. It was a nice day, late summer, the tomatoes hanging red and heavy on the vines in the garden she's grown every year for as long as I could remember. I was feeling good that day, telling her stories about Saint Francis that I'd read, describing his relationship to our family name. She pointed out a statue of him she kept in one of the islands of plants that dotted her yard outside the garden. It was simple granite, a robed man with birds perched on his shoulder.

The next day, we saw early in the morning that though it was late summer and past the bloom season, a trumpet lily had exploded in white over the shoulder of the statue of Saint Francis.

My mother had a painting of Saint Barbara that hung on the wall when I was a child. Saint Barbara was beheaded. I was never spared the details of her horror.

One day, in Queens, when Mya and I were still married, I was sitting in my partner Oscar's apartment and saw a saint card of Saint Barbara. I told him of the image in my childhood, and he told me that in Santeria, Saint Barbara was a stand-in for the Yoruban god Shangó. Shangó is not a creator-god, but a spirit called an orisha. Some orisha are descended from the heavens, and some, like Catholic saints, were once extraordinary humans with doubtful histories. The worshippers of an orisha are said to be that god's children. Though literal ancestors count for a lot in this religion, so do alternative family structures built on faith.

◇◇

My grandmother tells me, over and over, how when her sister Mary (named after Jesus's mother) died in childbirth, the blinds in her house all fell down at the second of her last breath.

◇◇

When I legally changed my name to Alex (a derivative of the middle name I had chosen in a church ritual, Alexis) my best friend told me that when she finally did all the name change paperwork after getting married, the person she had once been was gone. She no longer existed. She congratulated me on the formal occasion of my new personhood.

◇◇

The most popular (though not canonical) collection of legends about Saint Francis's life is called *The Little Flowers of Saint Francis*.

◇◇

Saint Alexis was born into a rich home, but renounced all of his wealth to wander the earth, penniless, a servant of God. After many years of wandering, he returned to his father's home, where he was not recognized by anyone. He lived with the beggars who slept on his father's stairs.

His father, his mother, and his wife failed to recognize him for seventeen years.

When he died, and his identity was revealed, his father cried, "Why have you treated us so cruelly?"

Before Mary's soul ascended into Heaven, she saw an angel. The angel would not relate their name, though Mary wished to know it. However the angel granted another of her wishes, like a jinn: the wish that she would see all the disciples of Christ before she died. They were dragged up to the clouds like in a cartoon and deposited on earth before Mary, marveling.

When Mary died, her body was surrounded by red roses and white lilies. Then her body, too, disappeared into Heaven. There was some blinding white light somewhere in there, I'm sure.

The night my grandfather, Joseph (named after Jesus's father) dies, my mom and my grandmother hear what sounds like footsteps in the bar next to my grandmother's apartment. She and my grandfather had run that bar for many years, and closed it every night at the same time. My mom and grandmother create a mythology around these footsteps: they were exactly at closing time; they sounded as if they were shuffling, which my grandfather did because of his bad knees; he was closing the bar for the last time.

◇◇

It is true that Saint Alexis's father, mother, and wife just wanted back the person they loved. So much that they could not see him in the person he had become.

◇◇

Shangó is a male god, but Saint Barbara is a female saint. Some marvel at the gender-irrespective transference, but most focus on the female saint and the male orisha's shared symbols—for one, lightning bolts, which were Shangó's favorite weapon, and which also struck down Saint Barbara's torturers.

◇◇

In the days before my confirmation into the Catholic faith, which happens at age thirteen, I recite, over and over the answers to the questions that the bishop will ask us on the day of. I choose the name Alexis as my new middle name, the name which is supposed to symbolize my acceptance, as an adult, of my faith. Alexis is a male saint, the patron saint of the homeless. I feel really wonderful that I neglect to mention his gender to the nuns preparing us for confirmation, and they never notice. It is a name I desire deeply, wish was my first name instead of my middle one.

On the day before we're confirmed, the priest of our church will rush in and tell us, so that we are "not alarmed," that the bishop presiding over our confirmation will be "colored." It is the '90s. I will lose the connection to this religion that day, when I realized I have more empathy for lives outside my own than a man who is supposed to be my moral superior, and my confirmation ceremony will be rote repetition that means nothing to me. The divide will only deepen one day when I find fliers in the church pews railing against a playwright who had the audacity to write a gay Jesus.

Shangó was once said to have escaped danger by donning women's clothes.

Sickness can be transferred into animals in Santeria rituals. These animals are then sacrificed. Animals who have absorbed sickness or death are the only ones said not to be eaten after sacrifice.

◇◇

The last day I saw my family, after my mom had her stroke and after I started to get better, as I drove back to New York City, heavy clouds broke into torrential rain, like in a bad short story, or a ghost story.

◇◇

Orishas only exist if humans continue to worship them. There is magic in the gods needing us, like aged members of a family need their children.

◇◇

Oscar has been taking care of his dying father for years. It weighs on him enormously. Spiritually, he may be Shango's offspring, but he would never turn his back on his blood family, or they on him.

◇◇

Relics of saints are only worshipped because saints are close to the one true God. But holiness can be transferred from item to item, down the line from the knucklebone of a saint, to something the saint once touched, to something that touches the knucklebone or the saint's belonging. There are whole families who revere a scrap of cloth that once touched a relic.

When I was growing up, my grandmother had a rosary filled with water from a saint's spring, something she would never have lost or given away.

◇◇

After I leave the church, I will wield the name of Saint Alexis like a weapon. It will transfer me from one life to the next. There is a certain amount of faith you have to have in this process, even if you don't have faith in yourself or anything else.

◇◇

To the best of my knowledge, no one in my family has ever been visited by the ghost of who I once was.

Conditional

I am living in Somerset, Ohio, a small town on Lake Erie, when Donald Trump becomes the 45th president of the United States. No one there will ever know me as anything but Alex.

I work at a small boutique resort. Somerset, outside of the resort I work at, is a pretty trashy place. It is filled with arcades, dive bars, people wearing hoodies that are hand lettered to say, "Keepin' it White Trash." Towns near Somerset have a different side, one where wineries abound, full of genteel servers and bartenders brimming with product knowledge and kindness. There are even a few places where I feel at home there, despite my obvious difference from everyone around me. The diner where the servers all know my name. The winery where I write and sip dry reds on the deck while snacking on a charcuterie board. The dive bar where the owner's son one day tells me a story of how he'd youthfully rejected a friend who came out as gay, and I tell him that it is obvious that isn't him now and I feel safer around him than most people, and he lets me behind the booth he dj's karaoke from to pick the music for the night instead of using the jukebox.

I am extremely good at my job as a server in the boutique resort. Going from restaurants in New York City to a small resort in Ohio is like going from fast pitch baseball to softball. I am able to focus on hospitality instead of numbers. I am able to incorporate my own life as a mildly successful writer into my table banter. The guests love me almost without exception.

Two of my most consistent coworkers are a forty-something woman named Ena and a thirty-year-old man-boy from Columbus named Brody. Brody tells a rape joke within the first week I meet him, and I hate him. Ena grew up in Somerset and is desperate to prove she is different than everyone else there. Eventually, because there is absolutely no one else, we all become drinking buddies. When they get drunk in the dive bar down the street from our job, they like to yell, "We're the best Somerset has to offer!"

Eventually, after several months, after the election of Donald Trump, Brody and I have drank together enough to get to know one another. I have come out as trans to all of my coworkers by then. Brody has revealed enough of his inner life to me that I know the frat-boy persona he puts on is just that.

"Just be yourself," I tell him over beers. "You're much more likable that way."

"I was myself for 19 years and no one liked me," he says.

"Now I'm this person that people respond to."

I know better than most that conditional acceptance is not acceptance at all.

◇◇

The resort owner's son is one of the few people who doesn't know I'm trans. He likes to call things he dislikes "gay," as in, "Who made that gay cake?" By then I am working in the kitchen as well as on the service floor of the restaurant. It was me who made the "gay" cake.

One day, he tells my manager, who knows I am transgender, that someone needs to tell me to bleach or wax my facial hair. She doesn't bat an eye as she says, "Alex is very proud of her sideburns."

My pronouns are not she/hers. I give them all the benefit of the doubt.

◇◇

Brody's grandmother dies the same week near the end of 2016 as my art hero Leonard Cohen, the same week Trump is elected. I happen to be going to New York that week, to stay with Adam, and I want to visit the statue of Saint Kateri Tekakwitha at Saint Patrick's Cathedral. Saint Kateri featured prominently in Cohen's second novel, *Beautiful Losers*, and I always go to see her when I am around Midtown. She had only recently become a saint after a great many years of being mired in the canonization process. Her final miracle was the clearing of a flesh-eating disease from a young boy whose parents prayed to her to help him. Her own face was scarred from the smallpox that killed her family when she was a child. Her sainthood, to many, represents the Catholic Church just beginning to make amends for the atrocities they brought down upon the lives of Native Americans.

I mention to Brody that I might be going there, and he and I talk about me lighting a votive candle for his grandmother at the church, who he says would have liked that. I buy a medal of Saint Kateri. I light a candle, and send Brody a picture.

I light another for my own grandmother. I light one for Leonard Cohen. I light one more, for reasons I do not understand.

Brody and I like to joke that we are AFFSs. Adequate Friends for Somerset.

◇◇

Ena leaves the restaurant for the slow winter months, then comes back when things are starting to pick up again. I make a joke about how her town's water has the Erin Brockovich chemical, and for weeks afterwards she talks about how she's begun ordering special water from a remote spring, and the health results are *amazing*.

◇◇

I watch as my rights begin to erode politically. When I talk to people I work with about my fears that it is the beginning of a plan to push trans people out of public life, they tell me I am paranoid. I rush to get my name changed. I begin stockpiling testosterone just in case a situation comes up where I or someone else needs it.

◇◇

Our new manager at work, a self-described affluent white male, casually talks about stockpiling guns and supplies in case a dirty bomb goes off in Cleveland. No one takes particular note.

◇◇

Brody decides that I need to learn how to shoot. I've driven by all the Trump signs that are still up in lawns after Trump's victory, and agree.

We go to a range. I am terrible with handguns, despite tutelage from both Brody and the girl working the range. I pick up a .22 rifle instead and begin to hit all my targets. Brody and I play a game of Battleship with a paper target, and I win. I keep the target. It is full of precise small holes from me and wild handgun shots from Brody. It is still in my car.

◇◇

About a week later, Ena, Brody, and I are trying to figure out where to go out after work to drink. I suggest a bar down the road where a guy I have matched with on Tinder works. I want to check the dude out with friends before agreeing to hang out with him alone.

"I'm not going there," Ena says.

At the end of the shift, I ask them again where they want to go. Brody looks at me and says, "We're not going to the bar you want to, and you shouldn't either. The guy's friends are all going to make fun of him for going out with a trans."

I stop moving as if I've been punched. We'd been to this bar many times before. I became hyper-aware of the conversation that had been going on around me all night, about the costs of friendship with or dating of "a trans." In that moment, and the moments after, when I go to HR, when everyone I work with stops talking to me until I quit, I realize that my entire life is, in some way, conditional.

Dating Apps

The first year I am on testosterone also happens to be the year I move to rural Ohio. "Changes in your sex drive" are a well documented side effect of testosterone gel, in my case the specifics of which are that I want to have sex 24 hours a day. This development, in the scope of living in a small, somewhat conservative town, is not a good combination.

Rural Ohio Tinder is full of people holding up fish, standing next to glassy-eyed, dead deer, and posing with their grandmothers and children in ways that feel exploitative. "Look what a good grandson/granddaughter/father/mother I am!" the latter seem to shout, while whispering, "Wouldn't you like to have sex with someone who loves their grandma/kids so much?" No, not necessarily.

Being from New York, I am used to a wide and comprehensive network of poly, kinky, and queer people complete with knowing who may have red flags, and having ways to check in on most of the people I may go on a date with. There is nothing like that in the part of Ohio I'm in.

Most of the gay men on Grindr identify as "DL" so there's no way to chat with their exes or friends about their past interactions and relationships.

My sex drive is ridiculous, though. I find myself exhausting the possibilities on OKCupid, Tinder, Grindr, and Scruff really quickly and looking at pictures of literal dicks on Craigslist. What's even more alarming is that I find myself considering them for a moment. My common sense kicks in before I ever meet any of them, but not before I respond from an anonymous email and a few cis men call me horrible names for not fucking them.

Around this time, I get in an argument on the internet. A man on a friend's page is claiming that young men can't be blamed for rape because testosterone is a "powerful drug" that clouds your common sense. He is half right—the latter half—but I describe to him in great detail how I've seen two sides of puberty at this point in my life, and while testosterone has made me think about sex much more and much less clearly than usual, it has never even once made me consider crossing someone's personal boundaries to get it.

Cis men, I decide, are full of shit.

Cis men say horrible things to me on Grindr. There is the guy who sends me a series of cryptic messages at 4:00 a.m.

after I have declined to meet with him in a golf course parking lot. He talks about how Trump is a Lamborghini underneath a coat of mud, but people like me are just piles of mud carved to look like Lamborghinis. I'm confused and amused. I'm less amused when I make plans to meet at a bar with another man, but before we meet, he sends me a series of shirtless pictures, one of which shows a tattoo of a Confederate flag. He claims that he's Italian and can't be racist, that the flag is heritage. I am terrified by the fact that I almost met this man in person.

Other cis men treat my transness as a fetish. "I've always wanted to fuck an FTM, it's my fantasy," they say. I don't identify as FTM, but I am frankly surprised the level of trans discourse has made it that far in rural Ohio, and I don't correct them. I also don't meet up with them.

I start watching a lot of porn around this time. I mostly watch FTM porn, a category that's not only easy to find, but really intriguing. I see things that are happening to my own body in it. I realize that the daddy/son fetish that a lot of men on Grindr seem to have about trans dudes is pretty common, and played up too frequently in these films. I also feel really great about the body I will have one day, and its level of desirability beyond fetish. I see Viktor Belmont's work, his flat, tattooed chest, and decide that one day I will not only have top surgery, but tattoo "When they said 'repent' I wondered what they meant" above the scars.

◇◇

I finally meet a guy who is willing to meet up, who does not disgust me, on Grindr. Against my better judgment, I invite him to my house. We don't know each other's names. We discuss the need for protection, and both of us say we are free of STIs. Somewhere in my head, years of hooking up as a female are telling me that I should absolutely not let this guy from the internet into my house. This is not New York.

Those fears are quelled by a few factors. I live next to a bank with obvious security cameras. I have a home security system on the door of my apartment. I live a block away from a police station. No one with at least half a brain (as this guy seems to have) is going to drive up to my house, murder me, and drive away. He might as well just stop at the police station first and ask them to arrest him.

He comes over. He's extremely attractive, just about one of the only guys I've thought as much of since moving to the town. We start making out and he takes off his shirt. He has an anatomical heart tattoo which I did not see in his full body picture on Grindr. A bell goes off in my head, the sound of which is dampened by the fact that I want to have sex immediately.

While we're having PIV sex, he tries to put his penis into my ass. He struggles with it for a minute, before I reach down and realize he is not wearing a condom.

"It just broke," he says.

This is an obvious lie. One I will confirm later, when I see the fully intact condom lying on the floor next to the bed.

I let him put a new condom on and finish, anyway.

◇◇

A week later, I can't figure out why I am incredibly depressed. I can't get out of bed. I want to die. The word "rape" has been buried so deep in my subconscious that I can't even think it might apply to what happened that night.

◇◇

I find myself at the emergency room. I have finally admitted to myself what happened, that I need to get tested for STIs, that my body has been violated. I think of the word Tai had once used to describe the horror of realizing that their newly feminine body was "rapeable." I feel, inexplicably, and irrationally, that this rapist has both affirmed and negated my transness. I feel confident he would never have done this to someone he felt was "male enough." I feel confident that he has put my "rapeable" body into a third category. The thoughts are confusing and probably not progressive, but they are mine, and they echo through my head.

The doctors are kind. They look genuinely hurt and shocked by the rapist's actions. They wince when I talk about bleeding. They offer me warm blankets, and do not press me to go to the cops, even though they try to assure me that nothing could have made the incident my own fault. They do not tell me about all the other people that he could do this to, because we both know.

My STI tests will all come back negative, thankfully. As if overnight, testosterone will not have such head-clouding effects anymore. Like every other person I know who has ever used them, I will delete all my dating apps for weeks before rejoining them, deleting them again, and rejoining.

A Better World

I have been in living in Somerset with my best friend, Sarah, for a few months before I go to the library. I don't know why it takes me so long. Libraries have always been my place of refuge. Sarah's home is also this space for me, a place where I am accepted in this small, strange town that is decidedly not New York City. But libraries are a different kind of sanctuary. They were when I was a weird kid spending time among the stacks with my friends; when I was an unwell twenty-something hiding out and reading Baudelaire and Rimbaud while sitting cross-legged on the floor in the poetry section; when I began to identify as trans and went to the small, nearby branch in Queens to request all the queer books from the main branch. It takes me months to find the Somerset library, to realize I might feel safe there in the way I don't anywhere else.

And I do, almost immediately. The person at the front desk, who pings my queer senses, doesn't press me to fill out gender on the application for my card when faced with binary boxes. There is a giant, orange-striped cat lying across a fake leather couch in the kids' stacks -- he is the library cat, Crash. I speak to another clerk about how I took a creative writing class in the library in my hometown as a kid. It had helped me become a writer. Do they do anything like that here? Do they want to?

She gives me the number of the library director, who I call up a few days later. She talks and talks and talks, telling me about the opioid epidemic in the area, the lack of resources, the illiteracy rates, and how art can save lives. There is another woman, a musician, who works with the library, who is doing her best to use art as activism. The library director has a fine arts background in painting. She is less extroverted in her activism, she says, but maybe this could be her chance to take a firm stance. And with me coming on, we will have a three-pronged approach. Her voice practically shakes with enthusiasm. We are going to do so much good.

We begin formulating a plan. I will work with kids from the middle school across the street, the ones who come to the library because they have nowhere else to go after school. I will teach them how to write short stories. I begin breaking the process down in my head in the most simplistic way I can. Plot, character, setting. We will have a workshop a week on each, then we will Frankenstein together all the parts. We will culminate the program in an open mic night where they can invite their parents and their friends to hear them read.

I speak with the director as I plan. Each time, she sounds more and more excited. Sarah, who is taking computer classes at the local college after she graduated with an English degree, begins building a theoretical webpage for a program called NEOPHYTE—Northeast Ohio Program for Helping Youth Through Education. We daydream aloud together, like we have since we were kids, about all the things we will do —in this case, starting up a local after-school program where we both teach. Her eight-year-old volunteers to help us by reading to younger kids.

◇◇

The library director shows me the flier one day. We have moved the program to summer, when I will have more free time. The slogan of the summer reading program is "Build a Better World."

◇◇

I get the call in spring. Do I know? Have I heard?

A man had kidnapped a thirteen-year-old girl and murdered her, burned her body. The news is reporting different things, but the one thing the library director knows is that the man had been connected to the library. A volunteer.

"Would you mind getting a background check done?" she asks. "All the volunteers will have to from now on."

"Of course," I say. "I've worked with children before, it's standard. And...also...I understand. I'm trans."

◇◇

A week later, in the days after I have been forced to leave my job because everyone has stopped speaking to me, I get another call. It is the library director. She doesn't want to lose me as a volunteer. She doesn't want to lose me. But the town of Somerset is so conservative—they aren't ready for someone like me to teach their children. I think of the things I have been planning to teach—plot, character, and setting. I say I understand.

Perhaps, the director says, I could volunteer for the summer at the local arts center, and when things have calmed down, when the man who'd killed the girl is in jail, when the world is a little better…

A few weeks later, just before I leave town, I stop into the bar where I'd almost gotten in a fight months before with a man who'd kept saying "faggot." I meet a man there who buys me a drink, an old army guy who confides that he voted for Trump. He doesn't hate anyone, and he doesn't believe Trump was qualified, he says. He wants to see the whole system crash and burn, all the corrupt politics come down from the inside; he wants to see the people who have always been held down rise up. He has a master's degree in theology, and we talk about the Bible, and what a mess of morals it is, how people cherrypick it, how if you did that you could find yourself justifying sleeping with your parents.

"You shouldn't sleep with your parents!" he yells at the

other bar patrons, in case anyone overheard us. We both laugh.

I begin to tell him about what happened at the library. I tell him about my writing, about my former plans to teach the children of the area, to instill in them the sort of love of books that people instilled in me as a kid.

"When are you teaching your class?" he asks, even though I have grown out my beard, even though I have told him I am transgender. "I'll bring my kids to that!"

I tell him how it has been cancelled, and why. He agrees it is a shame.

We get drunk, and the sunlight is shining through the bar windows and onto our whiskey. He goes back to talking to me about the world changing, and how there will have to be sacrifice. I know he doesn't mean people like him.

It is a shame, he says. But the system collapsing, it will certainly have casualties.

Genealogy (Part 3): Conversions

Mya's dad wouldn't come to our wedding because it was "intermarriage." He thanked us for not sending him an invitation and putting him in the difficult position of declining it after he made his feelings on the subject known. He was a rabbi, he said, and even his attendance would be something people would gossip about. He offered us a gift, however—classes meant to begin the process of my conversion into the Jewish faith.

I said okay because I figured it would make my life easier. I didn't really care enough one way or another to have or not have a religion. That is actually not true—I care a lot about faith, and I care about different approaches to it, and I care about so much about picking one that's perfect that I'll probably never do it. When I was young, I read about Buddhism and Islam and Christianity and even Zoroastrianism. When I was seventeen and supposed to go away to college before my nervous breakdowns started and threw me off track, I wanted to study religion and film. I wanted to find something that was so pure and perfect that it spoke to me in the way that I saw my grandmother's prayer book and rosaries speak to her. My mom, who didn't want me to go away to college, derisively asked me if I thought I would find some sort of truth. She said that all I would learn was that there wasn't one.

I had a lot of complicated feelings about religions. There's an aphorism in some Alan Watts book I read when I was fifteen that I've never been able to forget. It goes, "The centipede was happy, quite, /Until a toad in fun /Said, 'Pray, which leg goes after which?' /This worked his mind to such a pitch,/ He lay distracted in a ditch, /Considering how to run." I would think about it forever, but if someone else picked for me, that settled everything.

I met my best friend in grade school, but we got to know each other better because we were in CCD classes together. The classes took place in the basement of the Catholic church we both went to throughout much of our childhoods. Sarah had joined the church at around age 9 or 10 when her mom got married and converted for her stepdad. Our priest, a very old school Catholic, was so impressed by Sarah he often spoke about how he wanted her to be a nun when she grew up. Instead, she ended up leaving the church before even I did.

Mya was not a great person when I met her. She cheated on her partners. She made really bigoted jokes that she and her Brooklyn indie rock friends thought were hilarious, but which made me cringe, and which I slowly explained the insensitivity of over and over until she stopped. She said misogynist things all the time. When we broke up, she would say that I had been her teacher. That I taught her how to be a better person, the way someone taught me. The fact is, I worked really hard for every bit of knowledge I got ahold of. Mya and I had gone to the same undergraduate school, a small liberal arts, leftist one in Manhattan that she came out of debt-free and I came out of so far in debt I still haven't gotten out. She made it through without learning a thing about progressive values. While there, I threw myself into organizing and endured every mean look, every eye roll, every snarky comment of the people younger than me who'd been organizing around political causes since they were in diapers. I wanted to be a better person who made a better world, and I knew I had to undo so much of what I'd learned to do it. I held Mya's hand and forgave every lousy joke, every shitty comment. I gave her the compassion I'd had to fight for until she got to where she wanted to be, too.

"You practice *tikkun olam*," she told me, once.

Later, I would learn that *tikkun olam* means many different things to different people, but it will also always mean to me what she told me it did when I asked her in that moment.

"Judaism believes that each person has the responsibility to heal the world," she said. "It's like the Boy Scout motto about campgrounds. You leave the world better than the way you found it."

It sounded like the most beautiful thing, to me.

◇◇

Sarah's got a husband and a kid now. She definitely didn't become the nun our old priest thought she would. Sarah's zeal as a nine-year-old is something she now explains as, "I think Father John saw how willing I was to give my life up to something." That something became her family.

I had been in the church since I was a few days old, and no one ever suggested anything like a religious life to me. What I wanted was something perfect, something easy to commit to, something that made sense in the way the rest of the world does not to me. My mom, in some ways, was right. That thing does not exist.

◇◇

One day, I was baking cupcakes. This was before I learned to bake—I melted the butter instead of letting it soften to room temperature, and they came out dry and chalky. I was separating eggs into a small bowl, one by one, before putting them in a bigger bowl to beat.

"What are you doing?" Mya said.

"Checking to make sure the eggs don't have blood in them," I said.

"That's kosher tradition," Mya said. "Who taught you that?"

I shrugged. "I don't know. That's just what you do."

Mya began digging into my family history. It didn't take her long to find that the part of Italy my dad's mom was from is one of the centers of forced conversion of Jews into Christianity. These Jews (crypto-Jews, as they are called) often carried over "strange" habits into the present that they assumed were family quirks—lighting candles on Friday nights, wearing a red string around their wrists, checking eggs for blood before using them in any sort of cooking or baking. It was really the disguise an oppressed people had put on for so long that they began to believe their tradition was just inexplicable things their family did.

"You're a crypto-Jew!" Mya exclaimed.

"Okay," I said.

Mya kept putting off the classes her dad got for us for our wedding, saying we were busy.

Mya also liked to call me her *beshert*. It's a word that means nothing in the world could have lead to anything else. Inevitability, the preordained.

One day, I found out that a group of neo-Nazis linked to

the Golden Dawn party of Greece had moved into the Greek cultural center down the street from our house in Queens. I put on my coat and walked down, looking for information. They were paying members of the organization, someone told me. Later, when a group of local activists pursued the same question, they denied this interaction had ever happened.

I got home furious. But Mya was elated. She'd been doing more research. Donato, my paternal grandmother's surname, was a common name taken by converts, she said. And there was more. The rabbi from the time my grandmother's family had lived in Calabria shared the same surname as Mya's family had for generations.

I have always wanted to and failed to believe in destiny, in inevitability, in a spider weaving a perfect web.

Mya's dad stopped speaking to us when she came out publicly as transgender. Too many "irreconcilable differences," he said. So I never converted.

Sarah's birth father's family is from Italy. She'd always been told Sicily.

Earlier this year, years after we both left the church we were in as kids, years after we'd both given up on believing much, two years after my separation from Mya, years after I never converted, Sarah began reading a book her mom had given her. Her mom, Karen, believes in psychics, she regularly goes to card readers who talk about her two children. She always says the other one they mean is me.

The book is about soul circles. Sarah has really taken up this belief. She's been telling me for a while that everyone she loves is in her life for some reason that goes beyond this life or easy explanation. She feels it. She believes it.

Sarah saw her birth dad's family not that long ago. She asked about the region they'd come from, Sicily, and the sister who knows the most about the family laughed asking who told her that? They were from Calabria, didn't she know?

Sarah called me, ecstatic. She knew, she knew that years ago, our ancestors had been drinking wine together like we did. Soul circles. Destiny. A spider spinning a perfect web.

The great ending here would be that I dug deep, traveled to Italy, found how all these people had once been connected, and how everyone in this story must have been destined for exactly what they found—a link that had been buried by time and oppression and suppression and conversion from one life to another and a deep soul thread. That didn't happen. I'm a poor person, and so is Sarah. We like to chat about doing this, about writing a book together. She will write the bright half that believes and I will write the dark half that is reality and disappointment. But this will likely never happen.

I say I will write the dark half. But there is one more thing. At my wedding, at the wedding that Mya's father would not come to, Mya and I passed a red thread to each of our guests, then passed our wedding rings along it for everyone to hold and bless. The red thread, in addition to being a symbol of crypto-Judaism when worn around the wrist, is also, in other traditions, said to be an unbreakable link through life and circumstance, that will always bind people together.

In my best moments, moments full of hope, I think it would be hard to say I believe in nothing.

Letters

I can't forget about my mom. Is that even possible?

I dream of all the places I came from, spiritually. I dream of the pagan gods and the saints and the blessed people. I think of the sacred history of degenerate faggots, and the rupture that hurts us all.

Meanwhile, my mom, alone with my brother, gets older, begins to fade from life. She's in her 70s now, and I don't know if she's had another stroke since I last saw her. I google her name, occasionally. When my aunt died a few years back, no one told me until two years later. I am convinced the same thing will happen with my mother.

I think of all the moments she wasn't present for in my life—all the apartments she never saw, all the beginning-of-a-semester bustle she was never witness to, all the furniture she never helped me move, all the partners she never met, all the stories she never read, all the holidays we missed. What would she have said when I started growing my beard? What would she have said when I published a book after years of writing? What would she say about all this?

When I am moving to Cleveland, I open one of the boxes that holds all the ephemera of my life. In it, I find an envelope addressed to my mother. It was from back when I used to write her letters. I didn't even call, at first, for months after I left Wilkes-Barre for good, after her stroke. When I finally did call, it was on Mother's Day. My friend Michelle, one of my old friends from my anarchist days, came to pick me up from work, where I was in the middle of falling apart. We walked a few blocks away and sat in a nook between the sidewalk and a construction site. She held my hand while I dialed my mom's number, the phone number I'd memorized as a child, that hasn't changed. My mom answered. She cried the whole time I spoke to her. I told her about my life—I was living with people who loved me, I had published my first short story in a literary magazine after years of trying, was she proud? I promised to call her every Wednesday. When I got off the phone and sat there crying with Michelle, a man came by and told us that we were sitting in the spot where all the neighborhood dogs urinated.

The next Wednesday, I was locked up in a mental hospital, but I called, anyway. My mother never answered my calls after that.

But the envelope I find before leaving Somerset for Cleveland—it's a non-standard size. In it is the program from my wedding and a letter. I never sent them. I didn't think my brother, my mom's caretaker, would give them to her, so I never bothered. In the letter, I told her how beautiful my wedding was. How Mya and I had paused to recite the names of those who could not be there, her included. How all our friends had played music, how everyone had danced in the garden. How much I loved the person I was planning on spending my life with.

I wrote in big letters, because I knew it would be hard for her to see smaller ones. The handwriting looked like someone else's.

I never sent the letter. And when I found it, I threw it in the garbage.

◇◇

In all fairness, my mom tried her best.

In all fairness, she couldn't understand.

In all fairness, the time we walked down the street and I told her I was bisexual, and she told me that the bisexuals were horrible because they spread the gay diseases to the straight people, she was afraid. She had lived through the AIDS crisis. She had been so afraid.

In all fairness, I was so sick when I was young. So sick that very few people could deal with it. Very few people could see me through it. Very few people, even my mother, could have faith it would ever change.

In all fairness, after I was a missing person, she took me into her home, even though my brother who had lived with her his whole life moved out because I was moving back in.

In all fairness, my brother put in the money I didn't have

to buy me a car when I came back to Pennsylvania, after I was a missing person. After I left, he sold the car, and kept the money I had put into it.

In all fairness, I am sure I said awful things when I was sick. I had been so sick. Once, I had written a letter to my best friend about how I knew she was taking my letters from the mental hospitals and publishing them as experimental literature.

In all fairness, my mom told me many, many times that she had envisioned me as a toddler in a pink dress, delicately getting off the couch in our living room, delicately walking across the floor. That vision, I think, was more real to her than who I actually was. How can I dream of sacred visions and discount hers? I do, though, anyway. My visions reach to honor a past, and hers seek to replace a real, living human being with someone who she would have preferred them to be.

In all fairness, part of the reason I stopped calling, after all the calls that were never picked up, were the nightmares I started having about my family attacking me. Physically attacking me. Me unable to walk, to run away. Mya would comfort me when I woke up from them in the night, crying.

In all fairness, I was broken. We are all so broken. So many times, in so many places, we would have been foretelling a future, standing between worlds, burning some sacred fire that only we could burn. But now? We are (I am) so broken.

For Bobby, With Love

I first heard the story of Robert Evans from my mother, about thirty years ago, when I was five years old. Bobby to his friends, Evans was a gay man who lived in Wilkes-Barre, Pennsylvania. He was well-dressed, handsome, and gregarious, my mother told me. He lived with his own mother, was involved in local arts and theatre, was kind-hearted and generous.

"He called his mother when he wasn't home, every day of his life," an old friend of his told me years later.

My mother, not really one for humor, would always start the story about Bobby with a small office joke she played on him when they worked together, years before. She had taken a Kewpie doll she had won at a fair as a teenager, and placed it on his desk with a notecard that said, "Miniature Bob Evans." He was delighted. Years later, seeing his picture for the first time on a grainy microfilm newspaper replica, I would first cry, then smile at his tanned skin, small, perfect frame, dimpled cheeks, and brown-blond hair.

After telling this story, she talked about what had become of Bobby. One night, he had picked up a man in a local gay bar. The man had taken him out to the woods on the pretext of oral sex, and beaten him to death with a log. He'd robbed him of twenty dollars and the diamond rings he wore on his fingers. It took police a month to find his body.

My mother told me the story again and again through my youth. She told it to me when I was a young child, vainly trying to hide the long hair my mother insisted I never cut under a baseball cap so I would look more like how I felt inside. She told it to me as she pulled off the cap and insisted I was so much prettier without it, so much more feminine. Again and again, as she told me the story, I wondered if it was because she missed her friend. As I grew older, and the person I was inside years before I suppressed and forgot and fought my way back to who I knew I was back then emerged, I began to wonder if it wasn't something more.

The year that Bobby Evans died was 1986. President Ronald Reagan was fighting the war on drugs, but conspicuously silent on the plague brutally cutting short the lives of gay men all over the country. In 1982, when a reporter asked Reagan's Press Secretary, Larry Speaks, his thoughts of the disease, he reacted with laughter and homophobic jokes.

"[AIDS] is known as the gay plague," the reporter asking

Speaks about it had said during a White House press briefing. "I don't have it," Speaks replied. "Do you?"

The room was full of laughter.

In the *Dear Abby* advice column, Abby was responding to a woman upset about people's perception of her as a lesbian with her own timely thoughts on homosexuality. "Is one sexual encounter with a person of the same sex sufficient to label that person gay? (No.) Six encounters? (Maybe.) Is age a factor? (Yes.) Would a few same-sex encounters in boarding school make one gay? (Probably not.) How about men or women who have been incarcerated in prison for many years? (Any port in a storm!)" Wilkes-Barre's local newspaper, *The Times Leader*, printed a piece which studied 20 female sex workers to make the case that AIDS was uncommon in "sexually promiscuous heterosexuals." It was the gay disease. The gay cancer. Another article told of a local protest of a school that had allowed a child infected with the virus to attend. Anecdotally, a rumor had it that a wading pool in a local park had been shut down permanently because someone with AIDS had stepped in it.

Bobby Evans did not live in a safe time or place to be gay.

Bobby was the youngest of eight children. Friends described him to me as his mother's favorite, and relatives remembered when he was a child and the whole neighborhood would show up for his birthday parties at Kirby Park in Kingston. He attended Wilkes University, a private college in downtown Wilkes-Barre. Bobby's father, Stanley Evans, was a foreman at Dorrance Colliery, a mine that was operated by the Lehigh Valley Coal Company. Several members of Bobby's family were involved in local politics, and Bobby, at the time of his murder, operated a public relations and advertising agency.

"A lot of Bobby's friends were gay," said a family member of Bobby's. "A lot of his friends were dying of AIDS. People suspected things."

Thirty years after his murder, his relative hedged the admission that Bobby had been picked up in a gay bar with the idea that lots of people who weren't gay went there. I hadn't expected the phone call to be an easy one, but I hadn't expected his family members to still be denying his homosexuality thirty years later, either. When I spoke to a friend of Bobby's from the Little Theatre of Wilkes-Barre, I was told that Bobby's sexual orientation was no secret to his wide array of friends and confidantes.

In the early morning hours of September 13th, 1986, when Bobby was 47, he stood talking with friends at Shadow's gay bar in Edwardsville, PA, across the Susquehanna river from Wilkes-Barre. The dilapidated building that had once housed Shadows stood empty on Main Street well into my youth—though to be fair, all the buildings on Main Street are dilapidated. Main Street has always smelled like neglect and fried foods. Up until they closed in 2018, a Polish restaurant on Main Street had not given a single damn about indoor smoking laws, the air of their bar hanging heavy with decades of old tobacco. My older brother used to nudge me as we passed the former Shadows bar, saying that the lavender porch was how you could tell it was a queer bar. He did not use the word "queer" in the way I use the word "queer."

In a newspaper column printed shortly after Bobby's body was found, a witness that was there with him in Shadows in the early morning of September 13th described Bobby being picked up by a young man that the regulars had long considered "bad news." The man was later identified as Richard Kemmerer, Jr., a teenager at the time, though the full mustache and broad frame in his arrest photo made him look much older. He had recently been kicked out of his family's home and was living in a trailer park with his grandparents.

"Bobby was quiet, under control," the witness says in the article. "He was always under control, classy. He was always cautious about who he made friends with."

It's unknown what made Bobby abandon this caution that night, though the family member with whom I spoke thought it possible that the recent death of one of his brothers might have had him looking for some kind of solace. In any case, Bobby left with Kemmerer, and was not seen again alive.

◇◇

Bobby's family member said that the weeks that followed Bobby's disappearance were nightmarish.

"Where would he go? What could he be doing?" his relative said, as if reliving those days.

The family searched every weekend for his car, a cream-colored Chevrolet Monte Carlo.

When a pair of pants was found in the woods, Bobby's elderly mother clung to hope that he was still alive, saying he would never wear such faded clothes.

When Bobby's body was found on October 10th, 1986, Kemmerer was quickly arrested. Though his initial statement said that several men had emerged from the woods and killed Evans, after one and a half hours of questioning, he admitted that he had picked Evans up in the bar intending to "roll a queer." Kemmerer said he took Bobby out to the woods in Plains, off of Route 315. Kemmerer demanded his money, and Bobby fought back with a small blackjack he kept in his car. Kemmerer, according to his confession, hit Bobby in the face with a large section of cut tree trunk he found in the area. That confession, which he later withdrew, was written in a child's sloppy hand, full of misspellings. In it, he said that Bobby was still moaning and gurgling when he dragged him into the woods. He said the day after the murder, still driving Bobby's car, he went to a party where he showed a friend the rings he had stolen from Bobby's body. The friend said they were worthless and Kemmerer threw them away in the woods.

During court testimony, the Luzerne County Coroner

said that Bobby died from several blows that "broke every bone in his face." Friends of Kemmerer's testified that he regularly bragged of "rolling faggots."

"He said, 'Once you get them down, you don't let them up,'" testified his friend Renee Hozlock.

Kemmerer was found guilty of two counts of robbery for stealing Bobby's rings and wallet, but the jury was unable to reach a decision about second and third degree murder charges.

Ten people in the original trials' jury, it turned out, had been convinced of Kemmerer's guilt in the murder charges. Two could not be. Newspaper articles I found later told me that angry screams echoed out of the deliberation room. Kemmerer eventually went to prison for Bobby's murder, after a retrial in 1991 for the second and third degree murder counts. The charge he was eventually convicted of was third degree murder, which allows that something had happened that would cause a reasonable person to become emotionally or mentally disturbed. He didn't even have to say the words "gay panic," a defense that was once commonly used against gay people to suggest that their revelation of homosexuality warranted the crimes committed against them, including murder. Today, this defense has largely been done away with. However, a similar one, "trans panic," exists and is frequently used in cases where men murder trans people upon learning their transgender status.

Richard Kemmerer was sentenced from 10 to 20 years in prison, with time served for the years preceding his conviction taken off of his sentence. Bobby Evans' relative wrote letters to the parole board every year, detailing the heinousness of Kemmerer's crime. Eventually, the relative moved on with life, and stopped writing the letters. Richard Kemmerer got out of prison, got married, had two children, and went on with his own life.

◇◇

I learned that Richard Kemmerer had died, too, in October of 2015, at age 47. The same age Bobby was when Kemmerer took his life. Kemmerer died in a car accident, though details were sparse. I began searching, and found a post on Facebook that since seems to have been removed in which a woman who claimed to be his cousin said that he had left alone for a hunting and fishing trip and was not heard from again. His body was found on October 19th, dead from injuries consistent with his crashed car, in a creek off of Route 118 in Columbia County.

Almost thirty years after he had bashed another man's face in with a tree stump, then dragged his still-living body into the woods to drown and choke in his own blood and bone fragments, Richard Kemmerer died his own untimely death. That should have been the end of it.

◇◇

Bobby Evans' story has hung over my life, and in 2017, I decided to return to Wilkes-Barre to learn more about his.

Wilkes-Barre, Pennsylvania, is a town that was once made vibrant by the industry of coal-mining, but which collapsed when the industry did, around the end of World War II. The Knox Mine Disaster flooded most of the mines permanently, and what was left of the once-thriving city was decimated by Hurricane Agnes and the 1972 flooding of the Susquehanna River.

The Wilkes-Barre I grew up in was dismal. You didn't spend a lot of time downtown, in Public Square, the city center, unless there was a tiny arts festival or a farmer's market there. There was one place that young people hung out, a coffee shop called Mantis Green, which was closed down several times by public officials. There was another small show venue that hosted ska bands and punk bands. That was it. We all went to bars we were far too young to enter legally and listened to old poets lead open mics.

Though I grew up in Wilkes-Barre, I have barely been back in the last seven years—around the time when my mother suffered a stroke, around the time I began grappling with my gender identity and my older brother threatened my life for it. I stayed in the closet as a trans person until I was thirty years old. After I began to understand myself more, I thought back to childhood, to all the times I'd heard the story of the murdered gay man Bobby Evans, all the times my mother implored me to untuck the hair I had tucked under my baseball hat in hopes I would look more like a boy, to wear a dress instead of sweatpants, to be more ladylike. I thought of my teenage years, of the time when my mother saw a talk show where two people who I now understand were probably transmasculine had their breasts removed.

"Isn't that *sick*?" she said.

"Yes," I agreed, transfixed by the people on the screen. I didn't know. I didn't know anything about myself or anyone else.

I thought of all times I'd worn a tie or wished aloud I could be as androgynous as David Bowie, and my mother had stopped, shook her head, and said derisively, "Sometimes I think you wish you were a man."

I knew that my hometown was not a place where I could ever be safe.

None of us who went to high school in Wilkes-Barre in the '90s came out until years into college, living hundreds of miles away. In the early 2000s, a group of fourteen-year-olds chased me down the street, throwing rocks at me and screaming "dyke." According to an article called "An Examination of Hate and Bias Incidents in Pennsylvania 1999-2012," sponsored by the Center for Rural Pennsylvania, hate crimes increased in that time, even though overall crime rates dropped. Though legislation was passed in 2002 to protect LGBTQ+ people in relation to hate crimes, it was struck down in a technicality in 2008. In 2017, attempts were made to pass a "Blue Lives Matter" Bill that would protect the lives of police officers under hate crime laws. There are still no comprehensive state protections for LGBTQ+ people who are victims of hate crimes in Pennsylvania.

"I don't think it was a hate crime," Bobby's family member said to me over the phone in an uncertain voice. "But it *was* a hate crime. I don't know if Bobby…" Again, that hesitation. The truth of Bobby's sexuality too hard to say. "...people suspected different things. We didn't pursue it as such."

◇◇

    I got in a car and started driving on the 23rd of January. Rain slowed me down, and before long, it was dark, the rain had turned to sleet, and my anxiety was through the roof. My hands were shaking. I realized suddenly that it was my estranged brother's birthday. I wondered what he and my mother were doing at the house I had grown up in, that I never expected to see again. The last time I saw her, she was completely incapacitated by her stroke, and my brother had been buying her seasonal festive placemats for the tray she ate her meals on. I knew she was better than that now from reports my niece had given me while visiting, but I still pictured her in her wheelchair, eating some cake from a box my brother had made. Nothing probably would have made my brother happier than hearing his weird transgender sibling had died in a car accident. That was when I decided to pull over and stay in a motel.

    I ended up in a bed and breakfast in an old Victorian mansion, a place with plush white pillows, crisp linens on the bed, and a giant bathtub. The weather lasted into the next night, and in my comfortable room, I began making phone calls that nearly froze me in terror. I had wanted to learn about this man, about his life. Now I had to make these calls. I'd paid the subscription fees to an online phone book-type site, and dug up numbers for Bobby's relatives, Kemmerer's wife, Kemmerer's old friends. I called Bobby's relative first, and though I got no answer, in a few hours, my phone rang. We talked for an extended period of time. Bobby's family member kept repeating a detail that would haunt me. Kemmerer was much bigger than Bobby, his arms much longer. The relative recalled with loving detail the length of the sleeves Bobby wore on his button down shirts. Kemmerer had, the relative said, such an advantage over Bobby with his long arms.

I got off the phone, feeling destroyed. I ran a hot bath, and had just climbed in when my phone rang again. Naked and vulnerable, I listened to the thing that Bobby's relative had called me back to say.

"He didn't think Bob would fight. But he fought back."

That night, in the starched bed, tossing under a heavy comforter and the large, fluffy pillows, I dreamed that a man with impossibly long arms was attacking me.

I made it to Wilkes-Barre the next day. With the addition of a large arena and the strip mall called the Arena Hub near it, Wilkes-Barre had changed greatly in the years since I grew up there. According to many current residents, Wilkes-Barre's equidistant location between New York City and Philadelphia has made it a place where drug dealers who can't hack the competition in the bigger cities come to make their mark. The opioid epidemic rages there. In the Trump era, minorities often shoulder the blame for these troubles.

In Wilkes-Barre, I shuttled between The Osterhout Library, the courthouse, an old friend's house, and meetings with other friends. My friend Anthony, while we ate slices of deep fried pizza, offered to give me a stick and poke tattoo of a pink triangle. My friend Paul, who had grown up in Wilkes-Barre, told me how he was fixing up his house to sell it. He lived in LA, but his mom was still there, and he just wanted her to be safe. He told me he'd never experienced such outright racism as what was currently the atmosphere in Wilkes-Barre.

I dug into newspaper articles, unearthing names. I continued to make calls. I was amazed by how many people claimed not to remember.

"You're talking about something from thirty years ago," Bobby's friend from The Little Theatre of Wilkes-Barre said. "Memory is a little hazy."

I talked to the prosecutor from the case. He claimed not to recall it at all. Before I could question him further, he made it clear that he had to end the call.

I called Bobby's old high school, looking for yearbook photos, articles from the school newspaper, anything. Though no one remembered him, the current newspaper advisor thought it might be a cool project for the kids to look into. I never heard back from them.

I spoke to someone who had attended the same high school as Bobby, someone who had been a regular at Shadows gay bar. They all said it sounded a bit familiar, but was nothing they could recall details of. Many of Bobby's relatives have passed away by this point. Bobby was the youngest child, and the memories of those left have become indistinct with age.

And many people who *did* remember the crime did not want to be reminded of it.

I called the phone number listed for the woman who'd married and had children with Richard Kemmerer when he emerged from prison after finally pleading guilty to third degree murder in the retrial in 1991. She did not want to speak at length, but she did leave me with one comment.

"It never goes away," she said of the aftermath of her husband's crime. "You get pulled over for a traffic violation, and there it is. Anyone who has lived with something like this knows."

I called several numbers looking for Renee Hozlock, an old friend of Kemmerer's who had testified at the original trial.

"I am sorry, but I do not wish to rehash that," she said. She spoke to me via Facebook message—none of the many listed numbers were in service. After declining to comment, she sent me several chain messages about karma and angels.

"I don't think so," Kemmerer's father, Richard Kemmerer, Sr., said when I asked him if he would be willing to speak to me. "I don't talk about that, dear."

He sounded old and defeated. I had been terrified to speak to people who had loved someone who could commit such a vicious, hateful crime. I had steeled myself to encounter at least one unrepentant faggot-hater. But mostly they sounded as if the whole thing had killed them, too.

◇◇

 I gathered all the newspaper articles. I reached out to the people who had written them. I called the theatres, the gay centers, the people named in the news. I wanted there to be people who remembered, who told me stories about what Bobby's laugh sounded like, and that they could still hear it all these years later. I wanted to find a lover of his, or a friend, or anyone who could make this man real. The first time I found a newspaper article with a picture of him, I began to cry sitting at the microfilm machine in the library. He was short, well-groomed, handsome, everything I had heard but not seen with my own eyes. Looking at that picture, he became real to me—not a man in a cautionary tale told to frighten me.

 There were dead ends everywhere. And where there weren't, there was shame. Shame over the gay friend, shame over the gay relative, shame over the murderer husband, shame over the murderer son. Twenty-five years of my own shame.

 As I hit dead end after dead end, I thought of all the transgender people murdered in 2017—at least 26 reported, who were not misgendered in death, whose bodies were found—how the queer community I know attends memorials and says their names, how we refuse to let them disappear, how the internet holds onto their ghosts and memorializes them. But Bobby exists only in a few newspapers articles in a quiet library in a small town, in the hazy memories of those who have lived long lives, and in the memory of some transgender writer in Ohio who heard about his murder as a child. I think of that child, in camouflage shirts and boy's pants, that child who, in 1986, the year Bobby was murdered, had to begin hiding who they were. I think of the burden of being one of the few people who cares to tell his story. I wonder who said Bobby's name, what group of men who called him lover or friend had gathered in the places where they could find acceptance and memorialized him. I wonder whose hands he had held as they died, alone in hospitals, with everyone else afraid to touch them.

Somewhere between Wilkes-Barre and Ohio, I think of something I read long ago in a book, about how the first known AIDS memorial was to a man named Bobby, who had died in New York City many years before. It had been a simple pink triangle, the sign that gay men had been forced to wear in Nazi Germany. Above and below it had been the words, "For Bobby, with love." Hate killed so many in the days of this story, indifference even more.

Before I began searching, this man was Robert Evans, Bob Evans, a name in a story and a newspaper article, a cautionary tale that perhaps, on some level, did its job. Through searching, I discovered the man, the name his friends called him, that his relatives called him once or twice, with such affection, even all these years later. Bobby.

This is my memorial for Bobby. It's scattered photocopies and scribbled notes, phone calls from motel rooms, and drives in the night and rain. It's looking back at an old, dark era from the cusp of a new dark one. It's every one of us who ran home for our lives, and made it. It's every one of us who didn't.

"Why would you want to write about him?" Richard Kemmerer's wife asked me. I think she meant Richard. I heard, "Why would you want to write about Bobby Evans?"

Because he lived. Because he deserved to keep living. Because, even now, his sexuality is scary and inconvenient to so many. Because he died. Because he died a horrible death, alone and probably terrified. Because his death echoed across the life of every queer in that little town, every gay man who was only out at Shadows, every gay man who would never be out at all, every gender non-conforming kid, every boy in the theatre, every girl playing in the dirt. Every mother who looked at her child with fear, knowing what could become of them. His death left his beloved mother alone, and she died in a nursing home. His death seems to have haunted the man who took his life until he died himself, mysteriously. Because Bobby mattered. Because Bobby matters.

"For Bobby, with love," I write in my notebook, next to my notes, pulled over in a gas station on the way home. I write it again. "For Bobby, with love."

Acknowledgements

Earlier versions of these essays appeared in *Longreads* ("How to Disappear"), *Brooklyn Magazine* ("Georgette"), *Memoir Mixtapes* ("Hank Williams is Sacred"), and *Cosmonauts Avenue* ("Home in Three Meals"). Thanks go to the editors from these venues who helped form, publish, and promote a trans person's voice and stories: Sari Botton, Molly McArdle, Samantha Lamph/Len, Kevin D. Woodall, and Bükem Reitmeier. Additional thanks go to my editors, Michael Seidlinger, Janice Lee, and Esa Grigsby (who chose this book on its potential and patiently helped it come to its current state); the entire team at CCM; my closest and oldest friend, Sarah Baker; my nieces Scarlet Cummings and Bella Baker for giving me hope for the future; Rob Baker, for the Van Gogh cupcakes; my colleagues in the NEOMFA: Brigid Cassin, Jordan McNeil, Chris Alonso, Brandon North, Johnny Cook, Aimee Bounds, Elise Demeter, Mahmoud Kambris, Larisse Mondok (my constant workshop ally), Penelope Jeanne Girlblood (my sister), and Xan Schwartz (who shines unending light); my former writer's group The Stoned Crows (Joselin Linder, Mary Adkins, Christine Clarke, Alia Phibes, Nicole Solomon, Ilise Carter, Kate Tellers, Jorge Novoa, and Sam Ritchie) for wading through the early version of the "breakup album book," and other early, un-self-aware versions of these pieces; Hilary Plum for reminding me memoirs are not about evening scores; Caryl Pagel for identifying the book's main themes in an early draft; Zach Savich for showing me memoir's many possibilities; David Giffels for workshop leadership and for suggesting I occasionally let my voice crack like in all the best sad songs; the staff at Rising Star Coffee in Little Italy Cleveland for buying me gallons of Americanos in 8 oz. increments (especially Evan, who is not afraid of the dark); James Allen Hall and Sarah Einstein for their inspiration and kindness. A book is made by many people, and I am grateful to each of them.

ALEX DIFRANCESCO is a writer of fiction and nonfiction whose work has appeared in *The Washington Post, Tin House, Brevity*, and more. They are a 2017 winner of SAFTA's OUTSpoken Competition, and were long listed in Cosmonauts Avenue's Inaugural Nonfiction Prize. They have recently moved to Ohio, where they are still trying to wrap their head around "Sweetest Day."

OFFICIAL

THE ACCOMPLICES

GET OUT OF JAIL
* VOUCHER *

- -

Tear this out.
Skip that social event.
It's okay.
You don't have to go if you don't want to. Pick up
the book you just bought. Open to the first page.
You'll thank us by the third paragraph.

If friends ask why you were a no-show, show them
this voucher.
You'll be fine.

- -

We're thriving.

CPSIA information can be obtained
at www.ICGtesting.com
Printed in the USA
LVHW081129221119
637981LV00011B/433/P